IBC対訳ライブラリー

英語で読む
そして誰もいなくなった
And Then There Were None

アガサ・クリスティー 原著

ニーナ・ウェグナー 英文リライト

牛原眞弓 日本語訳

谷口幸夫 英語解説

JN090713

Published 2020 in Japan by IBC Publishing

Textbook rights arranged with Agatha Christie Limited through
Timo Associates, Inc.

カバー写真 ＝ © jelwolf - Fotolia.com (*left*), by klempa/Shutterstock (*center*), by editorial_head/Shutterstock (*right*)
ナレーション ＝ Peter von Gomm

本書の英語テキストは、弊社から刊行されたラダーシリーズ
『And Then There Were None　そして誰もいなくなった』から転載しています。

はしがき

　新しい本を手にしたり、未知のことがらについて調べるようなときには、今の時代、Google 先生や Wikipedia は、本当に便利な存在です。

　まずは、『ミステリーの女王』とも言われるアガサ・クリスティの生涯を、Wikipedia の記事を引用して、振り返ってみましょう。重要なところは、太字にしましたのでそこに注意して読んでみてください。

- 1890 年 9 月 15 日 イギリスの保養地デヴォンシャーのトーキーにて、フレデリック・アルヴァ・ミラーと妻クララの次女、アガサ・メアリ・クラリッサ・ミラーとして生まれる。**正規の学校教育は受けず母親から教育を受ける。**
- 1901 年 父が死去。この頃から詩や短編小説を投稿し始める。なお、**詩や小説を書くことになった理由は、インフルエンザにかかり、読む本がなかったからだという。**
- 1909 年 自身初の長編小説『砂漠の雪』を書き、作家イーデン・フィルポッツの指導を受ける。
- 1914 年 アーチボルド・クリスティ大尉と結婚。**第一次世界大戦中には薬剤師の助手として勤務し、そこで毒薬の知識を得る。**
- 1919 年 娘ロザリンド・ヒックスが誕生。
- 1920 年 数々の出版社で不採用にされたのち、ようやく『スタイルズ荘の怪事件』を出版、ミステリ作家としてデビューする。
- 1926 年『アクロイド殺し』を発表。大胆なトリックと意外な真犯人をめぐって、フェアかアンフェアかの大論争がミステリ・ファンの間で起き、一躍有名に。また、母が死去する。この年アガサは謎の失踪事件を起こす。
- 1928 年 アーチボルドと離婚。アーチボルドは愛人と再婚。
- 1930 年 中東に旅行した折に、14 歳年下の考古学者のマックス・マ

ローワン（1904年5月6日〜1978年8月19日）と出会い、9月11日再婚する。

- 1936年、『そして誰もいなくなった』を発表。
- 1938年 グリーンウェイの別荘を購入。以後、毎年夏の休暇をここで過ごす。
- 1952年 書き下ろしの戯曲『ねずみとり』の世界最長ロングラン公演（1952年11月25日〜）始まる。
- 1955年 MWA賞巨匠賞 受賞。
- 1956年 大英勲章第3位（CBE）叙勲。
- 1971年 大英勲章第2位（DBE）叙勲。
- 1973年『運命の裏木戸』を発表。最後に執筆されたミステリ作品となる。
- 1975年『カーテン』の発表を許可する。
- 1976年1月12日 高齢のため風邪をこじらせ静養先のイギリス、ウォリングフォードの自宅で死去。死後『スリーピングマーダー』が発表される。遺骸は、イギリスのチョルシーにあるセント・メアリ教会の墓地に埋葬された。

（出典：https://ja.wikipedia.org/wiki/アガサ・クリスティ）

　一読してなかなか波瀾万丈の人生だったんだなあと感じませんでしたか？　ミステリーの女王と言っても、ずっと順風満帆な人生というわけにはいかなかったようです。

　次に本作についても、記事から見ていきましょう。

　"本作はアガサ・クリスティをベストセラー小説家にした作品の一つである。同著者の最も多く出版された作品で、1億冊以上が出版され、世界中のミステリ作品の中で最も販売されたベストセラー本であり、2009年時点で『聖書』を1位とするすべての書籍

の中で6番目に多く販売されていた。本作の評価はクリスティ作品中でも特に高く、代表作に挙げられることが多い。

　「絶海の孤島」を舞台にしたクローズド・サークルの代表作品であると同時に、見立て殺人の代表的作品とも評される。孤島の兵隊島を舞台にして、10人の登場人物が童話「十人の小さな兵隊さん」の詩になぞらえて殺されていく。10人全員が死亡することで題名の『そして誰もいなくなった』を回収する。物語はエピローグに続き、警察の捜査では迷宮入りとなった後に真犯人による独白手記が見つかり、真相が明かされることで終結する。

　初期版の題名は *Ten Little Niggers* で内容とともに差別用語が用いられていたが、改稿を重ね、「Ten Little Indians」のタイトルを経て、1985年に *And Then There Were None* となった。"

　　（出典：https://ja.wikipedia.org/wiki/そして誰もいなくなった）

　さて、ここで Ten little Indians について、私の学生時代の思い出を話したいと思います。当時、私が通っていた大学の教科教育法（『英語の教員』になるための必修科目）の授業で、ある日恩師が「Ten Little Indians って知っていますか？」と学生たちにたずねました。なじみのある歌でしたので、私たちはみな、軽くうたいはじめました。

　　　　One little, two little, three little Indians;
　　　　four little, five little, six little Indians.
　　　　Seven little, eight little, nine little;
　　　　Ten little Indian boys.

　それから恩師が「Indians という言葉には気をつけなさい！」と突然言い出しました。「えっ、なんで『インディアン』が気をつける言葉になるの？」と、学生一同、顔を見合わせました。

恩師は、「もともと Indian は、Injun という単語を使っていて、アメリカでは 1940 年代ぐらいから、『黒人』や『インジャン（ネイティブ・アメリカン）』は、社会的にとても差別的な用語として認識されるようになったので、私たちもそういう言葉には気をつけなければならないのです」とおっしゃいました。

　さらに、その恩師は「One から Ten に増えていく 1 番の歌はまだいいとして、2 番の方の歌詞を思い出してごらんなさい」と続けました。それから「これは虐殺の歌なのですよ！」ともつけ加えました。

　　　Ten little, nine little, eight little Indians;
　　　Seven little, six little, five little Indians.
　　　Four little, three little, two little indians;
　　　One little Indian boy.

　学生一同、「えーっ、あ、ホントだ」と顔を見合わせて納得したのでした。

　さて、少し長くなりましたが、実はこの The Little Indian 『10 人のインディアン』の歌が、本作品の原点になっています。

　最後に、Wikipedia に、本作品の評価に対するすばらしい記述がありましたので紹介いたします。大切なところは太字にしています。

　　" The Observer で 1939 年 11 月 5 日にモーリス・リチャードソンは、「アガサ・クリスティの最新作が出版社をヴァティック・トランスに送り込んだのは不思議ではない。しかし、『アクロイド殺し』と過度に比較しても『そして誰もいなくなった』はアガサ・

クリスティの本当に恐ろしい最高傑作の1つと考えている。この作品を詳細に解説することは控えなければならず、穏やかな暴露でさえ誰かの衝撃を奪ってしまう可能性をはらんでいる。読者は純粋な批評が与えられるよりも興奮を新鮮に保たれることを望んでいると私は確信している。」と述べた。続けて、あらすじを解説した後に、「あらすじと登場人物だけを眺めることはアガサ・クリスティの作品を害する。プロットは高度に人工的であるかもしれないが、それは精密で、巧みに狡猾で、着実に構築されており、これらの燻製ニシンの虚偽（ミスリード）の解説は時に彼女の仕事を冒涜している。」と述べた。”

　一言で言うと、「ネタばらしはクリスティへの冒涜だ!!」ということですね。

　補足をひとこと。25年ぐらい前に、沖縄を旅行したとき、この物語と真逆の意味を表す沖縄のことわざを教えてもらいました。それは「いちゃりば・ちょーでー」ということばです。何度か声に出すと、「一回出会えば、ずっと兄弟・家族のように親しくなる」という意味がわかるかもしれません。読者の皆さんは、これから出会う人や書籍、新しい知識やその他もろもろとの出会いを、大切にしてくださいね。

2020年新春

国際エデュテイメント協会事務局長
達セミNEXT代表

谷口幸夫

もくじ

本書の構成

本書は、

☐ 英日対訳による本文 ☐ 欄外の語注
☐ 覚えておきたい英語表現 ☐ MP3形式の英文音声

で構成されています。

本書は、アガサ・クリスティーのミステリー小説『そして誰もいなくなった』をやさしい英語で書きあらためた本文に、日本語訳をつけました。

各ページの下部には、英語を読み進める上で助けとなるよう単語・熟語の意味が掲載されています。また英日の段落のはじまりが対応していますので、日本語を読んで英語を確認するという読み方もスムーズにできるようになっています。またストーリーの途中に英語解説がありますので、本文を楽しみながら、英語の使い方などをチェックしていただくのに最適です。

付属のCD-ROMについて

本書に付属のCD-ROMに収録されている音声は、パソコンや携帯音楽プレーヤーなどで再生することができるMP3ファイル形式です。一般的な音楽CDプレーヤーでは再生できませんので、ご注意ください。

■音声ファイルについて

付属のCD-ROMには、本書の英語パートの朗読音声が収録されています。本文左ページに出てくるヘッドホンマーク内の数字とファイル名の数字がそれぞれ対応しています。

パソコンや携帯プレーヤーで、お好きな箇所をくり返し聴いていただくことで、発音のチェックだけでなく、英語で物語を理解する力が自然に身に付きます。

■音声ファイルの利用方法について

CD-ROMをパソコンのCD/DVDドライブに入れて、iTunesなどの音楽再生（管理）ソフトにCD-ROM上の音声ファイルを取り込んでご利用ください。

■パソコンの音楽再生ソフトへの取り込みについて

パソコンにMP3形式の音声ファイルを再生できるアプリケーションがインストールされていることをご確認ください。

CD-ROMをパソコンのCD/DVDドライブに入れても、多くの場合音楽再生ソフトは自動的に起動しません。ご自分でアプリケーションを直接起動して、「ファイル」メニューから「ライブラリに追加」したり、再生ソフトのウインドウ上にファイルをマウスでドラッグ＆ドロップするなどして取り込んでください。

音楽再生ソフトの詳しい操作方法や、携帯音楽プレーヤーへのファイルの転送方法については、ソフトやプレーヤーに付属のマニュアルで確認するか、アプリケーションの開発元にお問い合わせください。

And Then
There Were None

Part 1

Chapter One

Sitting in the first-class train car, Judge Lawrence Wargrave smoked his cigar and glanced at his watch—the train would reach Devon in two hours.

Mr. Wargrave sat back and thought about all the news reports on Soldier Island. First, a rich American had bought the little island and built a large house on it. But his wife ended up hating the place, so they left, putting the island and the house up for sale.

After that, the papers reported that a man named Mr. Owen had bought the property. Then all the gossip writers started printing other stories: that a Hollywood actress had bought Soldier Island; that the house was to be a vacation home for British royalty; that the Navy was using it to conduct secret experiments. Nobody seemed to know which story was true, but Soldier Island was news, indeed!

■Judge 图《法律》判事、裁判官 ■glance at ～をちらっと見る ■sit back 〔椅子に〕深く腰かける ■end up ~ing 結局[最後には]～することになる ■put ~ up for sale ～を売りに出す ■vacation home 別荘 ■Navy 图〔国の〕海軍 ■indeed 副 たしかに

第1章

　ロレンス・ウォーグレイヴ判事は一等列車の席にすわり、葉巻をくゆら
せながら時計に目をやった——列車がデヴォンに着くのは2時間後だ。

　ウォーグレイヴは深く腰かけて、兵隊島についてのあらゆる報道につい
てじっくり考えてみた。まず、金持ちのアメリカ人がこの小さな島を買っ
て大邸宅を建てた。ところが、妻がこの島を気に入らなかったので、夫妻
はそこを去り、島と家を売りに出したという。

　その後、新聞によれば、オーエンという男がこの地所を買い取ったそう
だ。それから、あらゆるゴシップ記者がさまざまな記事を載せはじめた。ハ
リウッドのある女優が兵隊島を買ったとか、イギリス王室の別荘になるら
しいとか、海軍が秘密の実験を行うのに使おうとしているとか。どの話が本
当なのか誰にもわからない。とはいえ、兵隊島はたしかに噂の的なのだ！

Mr. Wargrave pulled a letter out of his pocket and read it again. The writing was almost impossible to read, but some of the words were written very clearly:

Dear Lawrence…it's been years since I've heard from you…you must come to Soldier Island…a charming place…so much to talk about…old days…bask in the sun…12:40 from Paddington station…meet you at Oakbridge…

It was signed "Constance Culmington."

The last time Mr. Wargrave had seen Lady Culmington was seven years ago. Back then she was going to Italy to "bask in the sun."

Constance Culmington, Mr. Wargrave thought, was exactly the kind of woman who would buy an island and surround herself in mystery! Feeling sure about this, he settled back comfortably and fell asleep.

* * *

■charming 形 魅力的な　■bask 動〔光などを〕浴びる、日光浴をする　■surround 動〔状況などが人を〕包む、周りに漂う　■feel sure 確信する　■settle back ゆったりともたれる　■fall asleep 眠りに落ちる

ウォーグレイヴはポケットから手紙を取りだして読みなおした。字はとても読みにくいが、はっきり見える言葉もいくつかある。

　　ロレンスさま……以前お便りをいただいてからもう何年にも
　　……どうぞ兵隊島へいらして……とてもすてきなところで…
　　…お話したいことがたくさん……懐かしい日々……日光浴…
　　…パディントン駅12時40分発の列車で……オークブリッジ
　　でお待ちして……。

　手紙に書かれた署名は「コンスタンス・カルミントン」。
　ウォーグレイヴがレディー・カルミントンに最後に会ったのは7年前だ。そのとき、彼女はイタリアへ「日光浴」をしにいくところだった。

　コンスタンス・カルミントンか、とウォーグレイヴは思った。まさしく島を買いとって謎に包まれていそうな女じゃないか！　そう確信しながら、彼は心地よく座席に沈みこみ、眠りに落ちていった。

＊　＊　＊

Vera Claythorne leaned her head back and shut her eyes. It was such a hot day to travel by train! It would be nice to get to the sea. It was lucky that she had gotten this summer job. It had come by surprise. She had received a letter that read:

I received your name from the Skilled Women's Agency. I would be glad to pay the salary you ask. Please start work on August 8. Take the 12:40 train from Paddington and you will be met at Oakbridge station.

Yours truly,
Una Nancy Owen

The address at the top of the letter read Soldier Island, Devon. Vera had read all about Soldier Island in the newspapers. She was glad to have this summer job.

Suddenly, with a cold feeling around her heart, she thought, "I'm *very* lucky to have this job. Employers don't like Coroner's Inquests, even if the Coroner did find me innocent!"

■by surprise 不意に　■Yours truly 敬具《手紙の結句》　■coroner's inquest 検視官 の審問　■innocent 形《法律》無実の、潔白な

ヴェラ・クレイソーンは座席の背に頭をもたせかけて、目を閉じた。今日は列車で旅をするには暑すぎるわ！　海に着いたら、どんなに気持ちいいかしら。この夏の仕事がもらえて運がよかった。それは不意にやってきた。このような手紙を受け取ったのだ。

　　女性職業紹介所から、あなたのお名前を伺いました。ご希望のお
　　給料を喜んでお支払いいたします。8月8日から仕事を始めてく
　　ださい。パディントン駅12時40分発の列車にお乗りくだされば、
　　オークブリッジ駅に迎えを出します。

　　　　　　　　　　　　　　　　　　　　　　　　敬具
　　　　　　　　　　　　　ユーナ・ナンシー・オーエン

　手紙の上部に書かれた住所には、デヴォン州、兵隊島とあった。兵隊島なら、新聞でいろんな話を読んで知っている。ヴェラは、この夏の仕事が手に入ったことを喜んだ。
　でも、急に心が冷えるのを感じた。「この仕事がもらえて本当に助かったわ。検視審問に呼ばれたと聞いただけで、雇ってもらえないもの。検視官はわたしを無罪だと判定したのに！」

The inquest had gone very well, she had thought. Even Mrs. Hamilton had been very kind to her. Only Hugo—but she stopped herself. She told herself she mustn't think of Hugo any more.

Suddenly, in spite of the hot day, Vera shivered and wished she wasn't going to the sea. In her mind she saw a clear picture: Cyril's head in the water as he swam to the rock. She swam behind him, but she knew she wouldn't be there in time...

* * *

Philip Lombard was thinking about the job he had taken on. Mr. Isaac Morris had been so mysterious about it all.

Mr. Morris, a rather questionable character, had offered Lombard a hundred guineas to do something odd. Lombard had needed the money badly, and Mr. Morris had known it.

"My client told me to give you this money," Morris had said, "and in return you will travel to Devon. You will be met at Oakbridge station and taken to Soldier Island. From there, you will be under the care of my client. You should bring your gun."

■in spite of ～にもかかわらず　■shiver 動〔寒さ・恐怖などで身体が〕震える　■clear picture 鮮明な[はっきりとした]像　■in time 時間内に、間に合って　■take on〔仕事・責任などを〕引き受ける　■guinea 名ギニー《英国の旧通貨単位》　■badly 副とても、非常に《need, want などを修飾する》　■under the care of ～の世話になって

検視審問はとてもうまくいったと思う。ミセス・ハミルトンだって、とてもやさしくしてくれた。ただヒューゴーだけが——だめ、考えるのはよそう。ヒューゴーのことは、もうぜったい考えないようにしなくては。

　そのとたん、この暑さにもかかわらずヴェラは身震いした。海に向かうのをやめればよかった。頭の中に、ある光景がくっきりと浮かんでくる。岩に向かって泳ぐシリルの頭が、水に沈んでいく。自分はそれを追って泳いでいるが、間に合わないのはわかっている……。

＊　＊　＊

　フィリップ・ロンバードは、引き受けた仕事のことを考えていた。アイザック・モリスの話は、まったく不可解なものだった。

　モリスはかなり怪しい人物で、ロンバードに100ギニーで奇妙な仕事を頼んできたのだ。ロンバードにはその金がどうしても必要だったし、モリスもそれがわかっていた。

　「依頼人からこの金を渡すよう頼まれましてね」とモリスは言った。「そのかわり、デヴォンへ行ってもらいますよ。オークブリッジ駅に迎えがきて、兵隊島へお連れします。そこからは依頼人が面倒をみてくれるでしょう。ああ、それと、ピストルを持っていってくださいよ」

"You understand I can't do anything—illegal?" said Lombard.

Mr. Morris simply shook his head.

"Well," Lombard thought, "I've certainly done some questionable things before and I've always gotten away with it!"

Now, as he sat on the train on his way to Soldier Island, he thought he might enjoy himself on this strange job.

* * *

In a non-smoking train car, Miss Emily Brent sat up very straight, as she always did. She was sixty-five years old and she thought the younger generation was too relaxed about their posture, their behavior, about *everything*.

Miss Brent was traveling to Soldier Island for a summer holiday. In her mind she re-read the letter that she had already read so many times:

■get away with うまく逃れる　■on one's way to ～に向かっている途中で　■enjoy oneself 楽しむ　■sit up 姿勢正しく座る　■re-read 勔～を再読する[読み返す]

「わかってるだろうが、不正なことならできないぜ？」とロンバードは言った。

モリスは軽く首を振っただけだった。

「まあ、いいさ」とロンバードは思った。「たしかに怪しげな仕事をいくつかやったことがあるし、いつだって、うまくやりおおせてきたからな！」

そうしていま、彼は列車の席にすわって兵隊島へ向かっているのだ。この妙な仕事、おもしろいかもしれないぞ、と思いながら。

＊　＊　＊

禁煙車では、ミス・エミリー・ブレントがいつものように、とても姿勢よくすわっていた。65歳の彼女には、最近の若い人たちがだらしなく思えてしかたがない。姿勢にしても、行動にしても、どんなことにしてもだ。

ミス・ブレントは夏の休暇を過ごすために兵隊島へ向かっていた。もう何度も読んだ手紙を、頭の中でもう一度読みかえしてみる。

Dear Miss Brent,

I hope you remember me. We met at the Belhaven Guest House some years ago. I am starting my own guest house on an island off the coast of Devon. I think you might enjoy staying as my guest, free of charge. It is a quiet place. Would early August suit you? Perhaps the 8th.

Yours truly,
U. N. O.

The signature was very hard to read. Miss Brent thought without patience, "So many people have messy signatures."

She tried to remember the people she had met at Belhaven. She had been there two summers in a row. There had been a nice middle-aged woman, and there had been someone named Mrs.—what *was* her name? Olten—Ormen—No, it was Oliver! Yes, Mrs. Oliver.

So Mrs. Oliver had bought Soldier Island! There had been so much about it in the news—something about a film star buying the place...

■free of charge 無料で　■patience 图辛抱強さ、我慢　■messy 圈乱雑な、汚い
■in a row 続けて、立て続けに　■middle-aged 圈中年の

ブレントさま

わたしのことを覚えていらっしゃいますでしょうか。何年かまえ
に、ベルヘイヴン旅館でお会いしました。じつは、デヴォン州の
沖にある島で、旅館をはじめるつもりなのです。あなたにお客さ
まとしてお泊まりいただけたらと思い、お手紙を差しあげました。
もちろん料金は結構です。とても静かなところなのですよ。8月の
初めはご都合よろしいでしょうか？　8日などはいかがでしょう。

　　　　　　　　　　　　　　　　　　　　　　かしこ
　　　　　　　　　　　　　　　　　　　U・N・O

　そのサインはとても読みにくかった。ミス・ブレントはいらいらしなが
ら、「まったく、きたない字でサインを書く人が多いんだから」と思った。
　彼女はベルヘイヴンで会った人たちを思い出そうとした。あそこには、
二夏続けて行ったはずだ。感じのいい中年の女性がいて、それから、ミセ
ス・なんとかという人も──なんて名前だったかしら？　オルトン──オー
メン──いえ、ちがう、オリヴァーよ！　そう、ミセス・オリヴァー。

　じゃあ、ミセス・オリヴァーが兵隊島を買ったのね！　あの島の話はずい
ぶんニュースになっていた──映画スターが買ったとかなんとか……。

"Anyway," thought Miss Brent, "at least I shall get a free holiday."

* * *

General Macarthur looked out the train window and tried to figure out who this Owen fellow was. He was supposed to be a friend of Spoof Leggard's. The letter had read, "One or two of your old buddies are coming—it'd be nice to have a talk over times."

Well, Macarthur thought, he'd enjoy talking about old times. Lately he'd been getting the feeling that others were avoiding him. And it was all because of that rumor about something that had happened thirty years ago! Well, it was no good worrying about these things now.

Soldier Island would be interesting to see. There was certainly a lot of gossip about it. But the train was still in Exeter! There was still an hour to wait. General Macarthur didn't want to wait…

* * *

■anyway 副 とにかく　■General 名《軍事》将軍、軍司令官　■figure out ～であると わかる、理解する　■fellow 名 男、やつ　■be supposed to ～と考えられている、～ とされている　■buddy 名〈話〉友だち、相棒　■rumor 名 うわさ、風評　■be no good 少しもよくない　■gossip 名 うわさ、陰口

「とにかく」ミス・ブレントは思った。「少なくとも、ただで休暇を過ごせるわ」

＊　＊　＊

マッカーサー将軍は列車の窓の外を見ながら、このオーエンという男は何者だろうと考えていた。どうやらスプーフ・レガードの友人らしい。手紙には、「閣下のご旧友も、ひとりかふたりお見えになります——昔話をなさるのもよろしいかと存じます」と書かれていた。

なるほど、昔話をすれば楽しいだろう、とマッカーサーは思った。最近、まわりの者が自分を避けているような気がする。なにもかも、あの噂のせいだ。30年も前のことだというのに！　まあ、いまそんなことを心配してもしかたがない。

兵隊島を見てみるのも、おもしろいだろう。この島については、じつにたくさんの噂がある。だが、列車がまだエクスターにいるとは！　まだ1時間も待たなくてはならん。マッカーサー将軍は待つのが嫌いだった……。

＊　＊　＊

Dr. Armstrong was driving across Salisbury Plain and was feeling very tired. With the success of his medical practice, he had become a busy man. He had little time to rest. That's why, on this August morning, he was glad that he was leaving London to spend a few days on Soldier Island. Of course, it wasn't exactly a vacation; he would be working. He had received a letter asking for his services. It had come with a huge payment! Someone named Mr. Owen was worried about his wife's health and wanted a doctor's opinion.

These Owens must be rolling in money, thought Dr. Armstrong. He knew he was lucky to be so sought after, especially after that terrible event fifteen years ago. He had almost ruined everything! But he had gathered his wits, and he had even stopped drinking. Now he was back on track.

Suddenly a screaming car horn brought Dr. Armstrong's mind back to the road. An enormous sports car rushed past him. Dr. Armstrong almost ran off the road.

"Watch out!" he cried angrily after the young man speeding away.

＊　＊　＊

■plain 图平野、平原　■practice 图〔医師などの専門職の〕仕事、実務　■little 形ほとんどない　■roll in〔金などが〕どんどん入ってくる、あり余る　■sought after 評判の、引っ張りだこの　■wit 图《witsの形で》分別、正気　■back on track〔人が〕立ち直って　■run off ～から外れる、横道にそれる　■Watch out! 気をつけて！危ない！

アームストロング医師はソールズベリー平野を車で走っていた。とても疲れている。医師として成功したため、こんなに忙しくなったのだ。休む暇もほとんどない。だから、この8月の朝、ロンドンを離れて兵隊島で数日間過ごせることがうれしかった。もちろん、本当の休暇ではなく、働くことになっている。受け取った手紙には、診察してほしいと書かれていた。しかも、とんでもない額の報酬が同封されていたのだ！　オーエンという人物が妻の健康を心配して、医師の意見を訊きたいのだという。

　このオーエン夫妻というのは、金がありあまっているにちがいない、とアームストロング医師は思った。自分がこれほど評判の医師になれたのは、もちろん運がよかったからだ。とくに、15年前のあのひどい事件のあとでは。あのときは何もかも失うところだった！　でも、それから気を引き締めて、酒もやめたのだ。おかげでいまは、こうして立ち直っている。
　突然、けたたましいクラクションの音がしたので、アームストロング医師はあわてて道路に意識を集中した。ばかでかいスポーツカーが追い越していく。アームストロング医師は、もう少しで道路わきへ突っこむところだった。
　「気をつけろ！」彼は、猛スピードで走り去る若者の背に向けて怒鳴った。

　　　　　　　　　＊　＊　＊

Tony Marston, speeding down the country road, thought to himself, "Too many cars in the road! There's always something getting in your way."

There were only a hundred or so more miles to go. Perhaps he would stop for a gin on ice. Perfect on a hot day! He began looking for a hotel as he drove.

But who were these Owens, he wondered? His friend Badger had found them and written to him inviting him to the island. Tony hoped the Owens were rich and would provide everyone with enough drinks. It's just that Badger wouldn't know who was really rich or not—he hadn't been born into money like Tony. It was too bad that story about that Hollywood star buying the island wasn't true. He would have liked mixing with film stars. Tony looked like a film star himself, with his six-feet of well-built body, his blonde hair, tanned face, and deep blue eyes.

But right now it was time to find a drink. He stepped on the gas and sped down the road.

* * *

Sitting on the train, Mr. Blore was making a list in his notebook.

■think to oneself 〔声に出さずに〕心の中で思う、ひそかに考える ■be born into ～ に生まれる ■mix with ～とつき合う、交際する ■tanned 形〈英〉日焼けした ■step on the gas 〔自動車の〕アクセルを踏む

トニー＊・マーストンは田舎の道を突っ走りながら、心の中で不平を言った。「この道は車が多すぎるな！　じゃまなやつばっかりだ」

　あとほんの100マイルかそこらだ。ちょっと止まって、冷たいジンでも飲もうか。暑い日には、それがぴったりだ！　彼は車を走らせながら、ホテルを探しはじめた。

　それにしても、オーエン夫妻というのは何者だろう？　友だちのバジャーがこの夫婦を見つけて、島へ行くようにと知らせてきたのだ。オーエン夫妻が金持ちで、みんなにたっぷり酒をふるまってくれるといいんだが、とトニーは思った。ただ、バジャーには本物の金持ちかどうか見分けがつかない——自分とちがって、もともと金に縁がないやつだから。しかし、ハリウッドスターが島を買ったという話がうそだったのは、残念だったな。映画スターとつき合えれば楽しかっただろうに。トニー自身、映画スターのような外見をしていた。身長6フィートのがっしりした体に、ブロンドの髪、日焼けした顔、深みのある青い目。

　でも、いまはまず、一杯飲むところを見つけなくちゃな。トニーはアクセルを踏みこむと、さらに道を突っ走った。

＊　＊　＊

　列車の席にすわって、ブロアは手帳に何かを連ねて書いていた。

＊トニー：アンソニーの愛称

"That's all of them," he said to himself. "Emily Brent, Vera Claythorne, Dr. Armstrong, Anthony Marston, Judge Wargrave, Philip Lombard, General Macarthur. The butler and wife: Mr. and Mrs. Rogers. Then, of course, there's me."

Blore looked at his reflection in the window. He was a large man, still in his prime. His gray eyes showed very little expression.

"I might be somebody in the army," he thought, but then corrected himself. "No, there's General Macarthur. He'd know right away that I was lying."

Mr. Blore thought some more. "Well then, South Africa! That's perfect. None of these people have anything to do with South Africa, and I just read that book about it so I can talk about it well."

Lucky for Mr. Blore, there were all types of people who went to live in the British colonies. He could easily make up some story or another.

With that settled, Mr. Blore turned his mind to Soldier Island. He remembered seeing it as a boy. It was just a bit of rock in the sea about a mile from the coast. Funny that anybody should want to build a house on it, but rich people were always full of funny ideas, he thought.

■in one's prime 働き盛りの　■lie 動 うそをつく［言う］　■lucky for（人）にとって 幸いなことに　■some ~ or another 何らかの~　■turn one's mind to　~に関心 ［目］を向ける

「これで全員だな」とひとり言をつぶやく。「エミリー・ブレント、ヴェラ・クレイソーン、アームストロング医師、アンソニー・マーストン、ウォーグレイヴ判事、フィリップ・ロンバード、マッカーサー将軍。執事とその妻のロジャーズ夫妻。それからもちろん、自分もだ」

　ブロアは鏡に映る自分の姿を見た。大柄で、まだ働きざかりの男。灰色の目にはほとんど表情がない。

　「軍人ということにしようか」と思ってから、考えなおした。「いや、マッカーサー将軍がいるんだった。うそだとすぐにばれてしまうな」

　ブロアはさらに考えた。「よし、それじゃ、南アフリカだ！　あそこなら文句なしだ。南アフリカに関係のある者はひとりもいないし、南アフリカについての本を読んだばかりだから、うまく話を合わせられるぞ」

　好都合なことに、イギリス植民地へ移住した人間には、さまざまなタイプがいる。なんらかの話を、たやすくでっちあげられるだろう。

　そう決まると、ブロアは兵隊島のことを考えはじめた。子どもの頃に一度見たことがある。海岸から1マイルほど離れた海に浮かぶ、岩だらけの島だ。あんなところに家を建てたい人がいるとは、おかしな話だ。まあ、金持ちは妙なことばかり考えてるからな、と彼は思った。

Chapter Two

When a little group of people had gathered at Oakbridge station, a driver stepped forward.

"Are you all for Soldier Island?" he asked.

The group, eyeing each other, nodded.

"There are two cars here," said the driver. "We'll take you to the boat, which will take you to the island."

The group made their introductions to each other and got into the waiting cars. As they drove through the country roads, each kept their thoughts to themselves.

* * *

The cars brought them to a dock, where a man was waiting.

"Are you ready to go to the island, ladies and gentlemen?" the man asked. "There are two other gentlemen coming, but Mr. Owen's orders were not to wait for them as they could arrive at any time." The man then led the group to a motorboat.

■step forward 前に出る、進み出る　■eye 動〜に目をやる、〜を見る　■keep one's thoughts to oneself 自分の考えを包み隠す[表に出さない]　■dock 图波止場、ドック　■could ~ at any time いつ〜するかわからない、いつ〜してもおかしくない

第2章

　数人の人々がオークブリッジ駅に集まったとき、運転手が近づいてきた。

「みなさん、兵隊島へ行かれるのですか？」と彼は訊いた。
　集まった人々は、たがいに目をやりながらうなずいた。
「車は2台あります」と運転手。「わたしたちがみなさんをボートまでお送りします。それからボートが島までお連れすることになります」
　人々はおたがいに自己紹介してから、車に乗りこんだ。田舎の道を走っていくあいだ、それぞれが頭の中で考えをめぐらせていた。

＊　＊　＊

　車が人々を桟橋まで連れていくと、ひとりの男が待っていた。
「そろそろ島へ出発してもいいですか、みなさん？」男は訊いた。「あと2人、男の方が来られるんですが、オーエンさんが待たなくていいとおっしゃったんでね。いつ来るかわからないそうですよ」。男は客たちをモーターボートへ案内した。

"It's beautiful weather for a boat ride," said Philip Lombard pleasantly as they all climbed into the boat. "The sea is as calm as can be."

Just then, they heard a car horn and turned to look at the road coming from the village. A beautiful car driven by a young man was speeding toward them. In the evening light, with his hair blowing in the wind, Anthony Marston looked more like a god than a mere man. But they would all discover soon enough how mortal he was.

*　*　*

As the boat neared the island, the house came into view. A beautiful, modern building, it stood on a cliff looking over the south side of the island. Fred Narracott, the boat driver, guided them onto a little beach. Steep stairs that were cut into the cliff led up to the house. As Fred tied up the boat, Philip Lombard remarked, "Must be difficult to land here in bad weather."

"It's impossible to land on Soldier Island when there's a storm. Sometimes it's cut off for a week or more," replied Fred.

■pleasantly 副 愛想よく、愉快に　■mere 形 ただの、単なる　■mortal 形 死ぬ運命にある、人間の　■come into view 見えてくる、視界に入る　■steep 形 急な、険しい　■remark 動〔簡単に意見などを〕述べる　■cut off 孤立させる、遮断する

「いい天気だな。ボートに乗るのにぴったりだ」船に乗りながら、フィリップ・ロンバートが愛想よく言った。「海だって、このうえなく穏やかだしね」

　そのとき、クラクションの音が聞こえたので、人々は村から続く道のほうを振りかえった。若者の運転する美しい車が、こちらへ突っ走ってくる。夕陽を浴びながら、髪を風になびかせているアンソニー・マーストンの姿は、ただの人間というより神のようだ。しかし、彼がけっして不死身ではないことを、みんなはまもなく知るのだった。

＊　　＊　　＊

　ボートが島に近づくと、邸宅が見えてきた。美しいモダンな建物で、島の南側を見わたす崖の上に建っている。操船者のフレッド・ナラコットは、客たちを小さな浜まで連れていった。崖に刻まれた急な階段が、上にある邸宅まで続いている。フレッドがボートを岸につなぐと、ロンバードが言った。「天気が悪いと、きっと船をつけるのはむずかしいだろうな」

　「嵐が来たら、兵隊島へは上陸できませんね。一週間かそれ以上、島が孤立するときがありますよ」とフレッドは答えた。

The guests climbed the stairs thinking about this unpleasant fact, but as soon as they reached the house, their spirits lifted. A very proper, tall butler with gray hair was waiting for them on the terrace. The house itself was very impressive, and the view was magnificent.

The butler came forward and bowed.

"Will you come this way, please," he said. The group followed him into the wide hall, where drinks stood ready. There were rows of bottles. Anthony Marston cheered up. This was what he'd hoped for.

As the group helped themselves to drinks, the butler introduced himself as Mr. Rogers. Mr. Owen, he announced, was delayed and would not arrive until tomorrow. He hoped the guests would find everything they wanted and were welcome to see their bedrooms. Dinner would be served at eight o'clock...

*　*　*

Vera followed Mrs. Rogers, the cook, to her bedroom. Mrs. Rogers threw open the windows and the sunlight revealed a beautiful room.

■unpleasant 形〔人・体験などが〕不愉快な、感じの悪い ■impressive 形〔景観や言葉などが〕印象的な、感動的な ■magnificent 形〔見た目が〕壮大な、堂々とした ■stand ready 用意ができている ■cheer up 元気になる、気分が引き立つ ■throw open〔ドアや窓を〕さっと開ける ■reveal 動〔隠されていた物を〕見せる、さらけ出す

客たちはそれを聞いて不安に思いながら、階段を上っていった。しかし邸宅に着くと、すっかり気分が晴れた。いかにも執事らしい、背が高くて白髪まじりの男が、テラスで待っていたのだ。邸宅そのものもりっぱな建物で、眺めがすばらしかった。

　執事が歩みでて、おじぎをした。
　「どうぞこちらへお越しください」と言う。客たちが彼について広い玄関ホールへ入ると、飲み物が用意されていた。酒の瓶が並んでいる。アンソニー・マーストンが歓声をあげた。これこそ彼が望んでいたものだ。

　客たちが思い思いにグラスについで飲んでいると、執事が自分の名はロジャーズだと自己紹介した。そして、こう伝えた。オーエンさまは遅れており、明日まで到着いたしません。お客さまのお望みはなんでもお伺いするように、そして寝室へご案内するようにと申しつかっております。夕食は8時にご用意いたします……。

＊　＊　＊

　料理人でもあるミセス・ロジャーズの後について、ヴェラは寝室へ向かった。ミセス・ロジャーズが窓をあけはなつと、日の光が美しい部屋のようすを照らしだした。

"You can ring the bell if you need anything, miss," said Mrs. Rogers. What a pale, frightened-looking woman, thought Vera. Her eyes darted from place to place, as if she were afraid of something.

Vera said cheerfully, "I expect you know I'm Mrs. Owen's new secretary?"

"No, miss, I don't know anything. I just have a list of the ladies and gentlemen and what rooms they're to have. I haven't even seen Mrs. Owen yet. We only came here two days ago."

"What strange people!" thought Vera as Mrs. Rogers left the room.

Vera looked at her surroundings. It was a nice, comfortable room, very modern, with white rugs. On the shelf over the fireplace was a large block of white marble in the shape of a bear. It had a clock set in it. Above that, hanging on the wall, was a framed poem. It was an old nursery rhyme Vera remembered from her childhood.

■pale 形〔顔色などが〕青白い、青ざめた　■dart 動 すばやく動く　■from place to place あちこちに　■as if まるで〜かのように　■surrounding 名《one's surroundings で》周囲のもの[状況]　■nursery rhyme 童謡

「何かお入り用でしたら、ベルを鳴らしてください」とミセス・ロジャーズが言った。なんて顔色が悪くて、びくびくした感じの人なのかしら、とヴェラは思った。視線をあちこちに動かして落ち着かず、まるで何かにおびえているようだ。

　ヴェラは明るい声を出した。「わたしはオーエンさまの奥さまの新しい秘書ですが、ご存じですよね？」

　「いいえ、何も存じあげません。みなさまのお名前と、お部屋の割り当てを書いたものをいただいただけなのです。奥さまにもまだお目にかかっておりません。わたしたちも2日前にここへきたばかりですので」

　「まあ、なんて変わった人たちなの！」ミセス・ロジャーズが部屋を出ていくとき、ヴェラはそう思った。

　ヴェラはまわりを見まわした。きれいで居心地のよさそうな部屋だ。とてもモダンで、白いカーペットが敷かれている。暖炉の上の棚には、クマをかたどった大きな白い大理石の置物。その置物には時計がはめこまれている。その上の壁に、額入りの詩が飾ってあった。ヴェラが幼い頃から知っている古い童謡だ。

Ten little soldier boys went out to dine;
One choked his little self and then there were Nine.

Nine little soldier boys sat up very late;
One overslept himself and then there were Eight.

Eight little soldier boys traveling in Devon;
One said he'd stay there and then there were Seven.

Seven little soldier boys cutting up sticks;
One cut himself in half and then there were Six.

Six little soldier boys playing with a hive;
A bumble bee stung one and then there were Five.

Five little soldier boys going in for law;
One got in Chancery and then there were Four.

Four little soldier boys going out to sea;
A red herring swallowed one and then there were Three.

Three little soldier boys walking in the Zoo;
A big bear hugged one and then there were Two.

Two little soldier boys sitting in the sun;
One got burnt up and then there was One.

One little soldier boy left all alone;
He went and hanged himself and then there were None.

■dine 動食事をする ■choke 動窒息する、息が詰まる ■sit up late 夜ふかしをする ■stick 图〔燃料の〕薪 ■hive 图ミツバチの巣（箱） ■sting 動〔針・とげなどで〕～を刺す ■chancery 图大法院 ■red herring 燻製のニシン ■left all alone ひとり取り残される ■hang oneself 首をつって自殺する

10人の小さな兵隊さんが食事に出かけたよ。
1人がのどをつまらせて、9人になった。

9人の小さな兵隊さんが夜ふかしをしたよ。
ひとりが寝すごして、8人になった。

8人の小さな兵隊さんがデヴォンを旅していたよ。
ひとりがそこに残ると言って、7人になった。

7人の小さな兵隊さんが薪を割っていたよ。
1人が自分を真っ二つに割って、6人になった。

6人の小さな兵隊さんがハチの巣で遊んでいたよ。
1人がハチに刺されて、5人になった。

5人の小さな兵隊さんが法律を学んでいたよ。
1人が大法院に入って、4人になった。

4人の小さな兵隊さんが海に出ていたよ。
1人が燻製のニシンにのまれて、3人になった。

3人の小さな兵隊さんが動物園を歩いていたよ。
1人が大きなクマに抱きしめられて、2人になった。

2人の小さな兵隊さんがひなたぼっこしていたよ。
1人が焼けこげて、1人になった。

1人の小さな兵隊さんがひとりぼっちになったよ。
自分で首をくくって、そして誰もいなくなった。

Vera smiled. Of course! Soldier boys, for Soldier Island! What a fun idea, she thought.

* * *

Dr. Armstrong came to Soldier Island just as the sun was sinking into the sea. As Fred Narracott drove the boat to the island, Dr. Armstrong thought to himself how nice it was to get away from it all—the office, the patients, the real world.

The first person he met after climbing the steps from the beach was an old gentleman sitting on the terrace. He looked familiar.

"Where have I seen him before? Oh! Judge Wargrave! I sat before him at a trial once," thought Armstrong. The old judge was known for having great power over the jury. This was a strange place to meet him again.

Mr. Wargrave thought to himself, "Armstrong? I remember him as a witness."

"Drinks are in the hall," was the judge's greeting.

"I must pay my respects to my host and hostess first," said Dr. Armstrong.

■get away from ～から離れる[逃れる] ■familiar 形 見覚え[聞き覚え]のある ■jury 名 陪審員 ■witness 名 証人、参考人 ■pay one's respects 敬意を表する、挨拶に行く

ヴェラは微笑んだ。なるほどね！　兵隊島だから、小さな兵隊さんってわ
けね！　なんておもしろいアイデアかしら。

＊　＊　＊

　アームストロング医師が兵隊島に着いたのは、ちょうど太陽が海に沈む
頃だった。フレッド・ナラコットがボートを島へ走らせているあいだ、アー
ムストロング医師は、あらゆるもの——診察室、患者たち、俗世間——から
逃れられて、なんていい気分だろう、と思っていた。

　浜から階段を上って最初に出会ったのは、テラスにすわった老紳士だっ
た。どこかで見たことのある顔だ。

　「どこで見たんだったかな？　ああ、そうだ！　ウォーグレイヴ判事だ！
裁判で一度あの人の前にすわったことがあったんだ」とアームストロング
は思った。老判事は陪審員に大きな影響力を持っていることで知られてい
る。こんなところでまた会うとは、おかしなことがあるものだ。

　いっぽう、ウォーグレイヴは心の中で思っていた。「おや、アームストロ
ングか？　たしか証人だったはずだな」

　「ホールに飲み物がありますよ」と判事は声をかけた。

　「まずは、ご主人夫妻にご挨拶したいのですが」アームストロングが言っ
た。

"You can't. They're not here," grumbled Wargrave. "Do you know Constance Culmington?"

"I'm afraid I don't," replied Dr. Armstrong.

"It doesn't matter," said Wargrave. "I was just wondering if I'd come to the wrong house."

Dr. Armstrong went inside as Rogers came out. The judge asked, "Is Constance Culmington expected?"

"Not to my knowledge, sir," said Rogers.

The judge's eyes widened, but he said nothing.

■grumble 動 ぼやく、不平を言う　■it doesn't matter 構わない[問題ない]　■to my knowledge 私の知る[知っている]限り（では）　■widen 動 大きくなる、広くなる

「無理ですな。そのふたりがいないから」ウォーグレイヴはぼやくように言った。「ところで、コンスタンス・カルミントンを知っていますか？」

　「さあ、知りませんね」アームストロング医師が答える。

　「いや、どうでもいいんだが」とウォーグレイヴ。「ただ、来る家を間違ったんじゃないかと思ってね」

　アームストロング医師が中へ入ると、入れ替わりにロジャーズが出てきた。判事はこう訊いてみた。「コンスタンス・カルミントンは来られるかね？」

　「いいえ、わたしは伺っておりませんが」ロジャーズが言った。

　判事は目を大きく見開いたが、何も言わなかった。

Chapter Three

Dinner was ending. The food had been good and the wine excellent. Everyone was in a better mood. They had begun to talk to each other more openly.

Judge Wargrave, influenced by the wine, was rather amusing. Dr. Armstrong and Tony Marston were listening to him. Miss Brent and General Macarthur had discovered they had mutual friends. Vera Claythorne was asking Mr. Davis about South Africa. Lombard listened to the conversation. Once or twice he looked up quickly and looked at Davis with narrowed eyes.

Suddenly Tony Marston pointed to the center of the table.

"Funny, aren't they?" he said. Arranged there were ten little china figures. "Soldiers, for Soldier Island. I suppose that's the idea."

"They're the ten soldier boys in the poem!" said Vera. "It's framed in my bedroom."

"In my room too," said Lombard.

■openly 副 率直に、隠し立てせずに ■mutual 形〔関係が〕相互の、共通の
■narrow 動 狭くする、狭める ■china 名 (陶) 磁器、瀬戸物

第3章

　夕食が終わろうとしていた。料理は美味で、ワインもすばらしかった。み
な気分がよくなってきて、さっきよりたがいに心を開いて話しはじめた。

　ウォーグレイヴ判事もワインのおかげで楽しげに話していた。アームス
トロング医師とトニー・マーストンが彼の話を聞いている。ミス・ブレン
トとマッカーサー将軍は、共通の友人がいることがわかった。ヴェラ・ク
レイソーンはデーヴィスに、南アフリカのことを尋ねていた。ロンバード
はみんなの会話に耳を傾けている。ただ一、二度、ぱっと顔をあげると、い
ぶかしそうに目を細めてデーヴィスを見た。

　不意に、トニー・マーストンがテーブルのまん中を指さした。

　「ほら、おもしろいじゃないか」と言う。そこに並べられているのは、10
体の小さな陶器の人形だ。「兵隊島だから、兵隊さんってわけだ。そういう
ことだろ」

　「詩に出てくる、10人の小さな兵隊さんよ！」とヴェラ。「その詩を額に
入れて、わたしの寝室に飾ってあるわ」

　「おれの部屋にもあるよ」とロンバード。

"And mine."

Everybody said the same.

"It's a fun idea, isn't it?" said Vera.

"Very childish," said Wargrave as he poured himself more wine.

The party moved to the drawing room. The French windows were open, and the sound of the sea floated in. The guests made small talk with each other as Rogers served coffee. The coffee was very good—black and hot.

Into this comfortable scene suddenly came The Voice. It came without warning, shattering the peace:

"Ladies and gentlemen! Silence please!"

Everyone looked at each other in surprise. Who was speaking? The Voice continued:

■drawing room 応接間、客間　■small talk 世間話、雑談　■without warning〔好ましくない出来事などが〕何の前触れもなく　■shatter 動～を打ち砕く、台なしにする

「わたしの部屋にもありますよ」

みなが口をそろえた。

「おもしろいアイデアよね」とヴェラ。

「ふん、子どもじみた真似だ」ウォーグレイヴは、さらにワインをつぎながら言った。

パーティーは客間へ移った。フランス窓があいているので、波の音が漂ってくる。客たちは世間話に花を咲かせ、ロジャーズがコーヒーを配っている。とても味のいい、熱々のブラックコーヒー。

この心地よい場に、突然、「声」が響いてきたのだ。なんの前触れもなく襲ってきて、平和を打ち砕いた。

「みなさん！　お静かに！」

みんなはびっくりして、たがいに見つめあった。いったい誰が話しているのだろう？　「声」は続いた。

"You are charged with the following crimes:

"Edward Armstrong, you caused the death of Louisa Mary Clees on March 14, 1925.

"Emily Brent, you were responsible for the death of Beatrice Taylor on November 5, 1931.

"William Blore, you brought about the death of James Landor on October 10, 1928.

"Vera Claythorne, you killed Cyril Hamilton on August 11, 1935.

"Philip Lombard, on a day in February 1932, you were guilty of the death of twenty-one men who were members of an East African tribe.

"John Macarthur, on January 4, 1917, you sent your wife's lover, Arthur Richmond, to his death.

"Anthony Marston, on November 14th of last year, you murdered John and Lucy Combes.

"Thomas Rogers and Ethel Rogers, you brought about the death of Jennifer Brady on May 6, 1929.

"Lawrence Wargrave, you were guilty of the murder of Edward Seton on June 10, 1930.

"Prisoners, have you anything to say in your defense?"

■be charged with ～の罪で告発される ■be responsible for ～に対して責任がある
■bring about 〔徐々に〕～をもたらす ■be guilty of ～の罪を犯している
■prisoner 名 被告人 ■in defense ～を擁護しようとして

「あなたたちは次に述べる罪状で告発されている」

「エドワード・アームストロング、あなたは1925年3月14日、ルイーザ・メアリ・クリースを死に至らしめた」

「エミリー・ブレント、あなたは1931年11月5日、ビアトリス・テイラーの死に関与した」

「ウィリアム・ブロア、あなたは1928年10月10日、ジェイムズ・ランドーを死に至らしめた」

「ヴェラ・クレイソーン、あなたは1935年8月11日、シリル・ハミルトンを殺害した」

「フィリップ・ロンバード、あなたは1932年2月のある日、東アフリカの部族民21名を死に至らしめた」

「ジョン・マッカーサー、あなたは1917年1月4日、妻の愛人アーサー・リッチモンドを死地へ送った」

「アンソニー・マーストン、あなたは昨年の11月14日、ジョンならびにルーシー・コームズを殺害した」

「トーマス・ロジャーズ、ならびにエセル・ロジャーズ、あなたたちは1929年5月6日、ジェニファー・ブレイディーを死に至らしめた」

「ロレンス・ウォーグレイヴ、あなたは1930年6月10日、エドワード・シートンを殺害した」

「被告人たちよ、何か申し開きができるか？」

∗　∗　∗

The Voice stopped. There was a great crash as Rogers dropped the coffee tray. From outside the room came a scream and a thud.

Lombard ran to the door and found Mrs. Rogers lying in the hall. Tony Marston helped him move the woman to the sofa in the drawing room. Dr. Armstrong came over quickly to examine her.

"She's fine," he said. "She just fainted." He told Rogers to get some brandy. As Rogers, his face white and his hands shaking, left the room, Vera cried out, "Who was that speaking? Where is he?"

"What's going on here?" joined in General Macarthur.

"That voice sounded like it was in the room," said Lombard, his eyes moving around the walls. He suddenly moved to a door near the fireplace and threw the door open. Inside the next room was a table with a record player on it.

"Here it is!" he said. All the others crowded after him. Only Miss Brent stayed sitting in her chair.

■thud 图 ドサッという音《鈍い衝撃音》　■lie 動〔人などがある場所に〕横たわる
■examine 動〔患者の健康状態を〕検査[診察]する　■faint 動 気絶する、失神する
■crowd 動 押し寄せる、群がる

　　　　　　　　　　　　　　　＊　＊　＊

　「声」はやんだ。ロジャーズがコーヒーの盆を落とし、すさまじい音をた
てた。部屋の外から悲鳴が聞こえ、ドサッという音がする。

　ロンバードが戸口へ駆けよると、ミセス・ロジャーズがホールで倒れて
いた。トニー・マーストンが手伝い、彼女を客間のソファへ運んだ。アー
ムストロング医師がすばやく近づいて具合をみる。

　「大丈夫。気を失っただけです」そしてロジャーズに、ブランデーを持っ
てくるように言った。真っ青な顔で、手を震わせたロジャーズが部屋から
出ていくと、ヴェラが叫んだ。「誰が話してたの？　どこにいるの？」

　「いったい何が起こってるんだ？」マッカーサー将軍も言った。
　「あの声は部屋の中から聞こえたようだったな」ロンバードがそう言っ
て、壁じゅうに目を走らせた。そしていきなり暖炉わきのドアへ向かうと、
ドアをあけはなった。すると隣室に、レコードプレーヤーを置いたテーブ
ルがあったのだ。
　「あったぞ！」と彼が言うと、他の者たちがいっせいに後からついていっ
た。ミス・ブレントだけが椅子にじっとすわっていた。

Inside the room, the record player and table was moved up close against the wall. Lombard found two or three small holes that had been made in the wall to let the sound through into the drawing room. He placed the needle on the record and immediately, they heard again,

"You are charged with the following crimes—"

"Turn it off!" cried Vera.

Dr. Armstrong said with some relief, "I suppose it's just a terrible joke."

"But who turned it on?" asked Marston.

"Yes," said the judge. "Let's find out." He led the way back into the drawing room.

Rogers had just come in with the brandy, and Miss Brent was helping Mrs. Rogers sit up.

"Ethel, you're all right. Everything is all right. You must pull yourself together," Rogers was saying to his wife.

"Mrs. Rogers, you just had a bad shock," said Dr. Armstrong. Turning to Rogers, he demanded, "Where's that brandy?"

Rogers had set it down on a nearby table. The doctor handed it to Mrs. Rogers. She drank a little, and it seemed to do her good.

■immediately 副〜するとすぐに ■pull oneself together 自分を取り戻す、立ち直る ■demand 動〔必要なものを〕求める、〜を必要とする ■do ~ good 〜に効果がある〔役に立つ〕、〜のためになる

その部屋では、レコードプレーヤーを置いたテーブルが壁のすぐそばに寄せられていた。ロンバートが調べると、客間まで音が通るように、壁に2、3個の小さな穴があけられていた。針をレコードに当てたとたん、あの声がふたたび響いた。

「あなたたちは次に述べる罪状で告発されている──」

　「とめて！」ヴェラが叫んだ。
　アームストロング医師がいくらか安心したように言った。「ただの悪質ないたずらですね」
　「でも、だれがレコードをかけたんです？」マーストンが訊いた。
　「そのとおりだ」と判事。「それを調べようではないか」彼は客間へ戻っていった。
　そこへロジャーズがブランデーを持って入ってきたので、ミス・ブレントがミセス・ロジャーズを支えてすわらせた。
　「エセル、大丈夫だよ。何も問題ない。しっかりするんだ」ロジャーズが妻に声をかけた。
　「奥さん、ひどくショックを受けただけですよ」とアームストロング医師は言い、ロジャーズに尋ねた。「ブランデーはどこだい？」
　ロジャーズはブランデーのグラスをそばのテーブルに置いていた。医師がそれを取って、ミセス・ロジャーズに渡した。彼女が少し飲むと、効き目が表れてきたようだった。

"She's feeling much better now, thank you doctor," said Rogers. "I was quite shocked too, I dropped my tray—"

He was interrupted by Judge Wargrave. "Who put that record on?" the judge asked Rogers. "Was it you?"

"I had no idea what it was!" cried Rogers. "I was just obeying orders, sir!"

"You'd better explain," said the judge.

"Mr. Owen told me to play a record. He said I'd find the record in the room there, and my wife was to put it on as I served coffee in the drawing room. That's the truth, I swear!"

"That's ridiculous!" burst out General Macarthur. "This Owen, whoever he is—"

"But who *is* he?" asked Miss Brent.

"That is exactly what we must figure out," said the judge. "Rogers, I suggest you take your wife to her bed first. Then come back here."

"I'll give you a hand," said Dr. Armstrong.

The two men led Mrs. Rogers out of the room.

"I could use a drink," said Tony when they had gone. The others, except for Miss Brent, agreed, and everyone poured a drink. Soon Dr. Armstrong returned.

■interrupt 動（人）の言葉を遮る、割って入る　■have no idea 全くわからない
■obey 動〜に従う　■had better 〜したほうが身のためだ《省略形 'd better》
■I swear. 本当です。誓います。　■ridiculous 形ばかげた、おかしな　■burst out〔感情を〕急に表す、激発する　■give someone a hand （人）に手を貸す、（人）を助ける［手伝う］

「ずいぶんよくなったようです。ありがとうございました、先生」とロジャーズ。「わたしもひどくショックを受けました。それでお盆を落としたりして——」

ウォーグレイヴ判事がそれをさえぎった。「誰がレコードをかけたのかね?」とロジャーズに訊いた。「きみなのか?」

「どんなレコードか知らなかったのです!」ロジャーズは声をあげた。「わたしはただご指示に従っただけです!」

「説明してもらおうか」と判事。

「オーエンさまが、レコードをかけるようにとおっしゃったのです。その部屋にレコードがあるからと。わたしが客間でコーヒーをお出ししている間に、妻がかけることになっておりました。本当です、神に誓います!」

「まったく馬鹿げておる!」マッカーサー将軍が怒りだした。「このオーエンとかいう男、どんなやつか知らんが——」

「でも、いったい、どういう人なんです?」ミス・ブレントが訊いた。

「それこそ、はっきりさせねばならんな」と判事は言った。「ロジャーズ、まずは奥さんをベッドに寝かせてくるといい。それから戻ってきてくれ」

「手伝うよ」とアームストロング医師。

ふたりはミセス・ロジャーズを部屋から連れだした。

「ぼくは一杯飲みたいな」彼らが出ていくと、トニーが言った。ミス・ブレント以外のみながそれに賛成し、それぞれ飲み物をついだ。まもなく、アームストロング医師が戻ってきた。

"She's all right," he said. "I gave her sleeping medicine. And I'll take a drink, too." A moment later, Rogers also returned. Then Wargrave took charge. The room suddenly became a court of law.

"Now, Rogers, I want you to tell us what you know of this Mr. Owen."

"Well, I can't, sir. I've never met him. My wife and I have only been here a few days. We were hired by letter, through the Regina Agency in Plymouth."

"A well-respected agency," said Mr. Blore, nodding.

"We were to arrive on a certain day," continued Rogers. "Everything was in order here—plenty of food in stock, everything nice. Then we got orders—by letter again—to prepare for a house party. Yesterday I got a message from Mr. Owen saying he and his wife had been delayed and to carry on as best as we could. He gave instructions about dinner and coffee and putting on the record."

"Surely you have that letter," said the judge.

"I do," said Rogers, taking it out of his pocket and giving it to Wargrave.

■take charge 支配する、実権を握る　■court of law 法廷、裁判所　■well-respected とても信用のある、大変評判の高い　■in order 整って、整頓されて　■plenty of たくさんの　■in stock 在庫の、買い置きの

「彼女は大丈夫ですよ。睡眠薬をあげてきました。おや、わたしも一杯いただこうかな」少したって、ロジャーズも戻ってきた。すると、ウォーグレイヴが指揮をとった。客間は突然、法廷に変わったのだ。

　「さて、ロジャーズ、このオーエンという人物について、知っていることを話してもらいたい」
　「そのう、それができないのでございます。まだお目にかかったことがありませんので。妻とわたしは数日前にここへ来たところです。プリマスのレジャイナ・エージェンシーを通して、お手紙で雇われたのです」
　「とても信用のある紹介所ですね」ブロアがうなずきながら言った。
　「指定された日に来ることになっておりました」ロジャーズは続けた。「ここへ着くと、何もかもが整っておりました——食料品はたくさん買い置かれておりましたし、あらゆるものが立派でした。それから、パーティーの用意をするようにとのご指示がありました——これもお手紙によるものです。昨日もオーエンさまからご連絡があり、オーエンさまと奥さまは遅れるので、わたしたちでできるかぎり、おもてなしするようにとのことでした。そして夕食とコーヒーと、レコードをかけることについてご指示を受けたのでございます」
　「その手紙を持っているだろうね」判事が言った。
　「はい、持っております」とロジャーズは言うと、ポケットから手紙を取りだして、ウォーグレイヴに渡した。

"Hmm," said the judge. "It's typewritten and made out from the Ritz Hotel."

"He's got some fancy names, doesn't he?" remarked Tony, looking over the judge's shoulder. "Ulick Norman Owen."

"Thank you, Marston, for pointing that out," said the judge. "I believe it's time for us to share all the information we have about our host. We are all his guests. How were we invited here?"

Miss Brent spoke first. "I received a letter from a woman who said we'd met two or three years ago. The signature was hard to read. I thought it said Oliver, or perhaps Ogden. I know a Mrs. Oliver and also a Miss Ogden. But I'm sure I don't know anyone named Owen."

Miss Brent took the letter from her pocket and showed it to the judge.

"Miss Claythorne?" he said, turning to the young lady.

Vera explained how she was employed as Mrs. Owen's secretary.

"Marston?" said the judge.

■typewritten 形 タイプライターで打った ■make out 作成する、書き上げる
■fancy 形 風変わりな ■I'm sure ~. ~は確かです。きっと~です。

「ふうむ」と判事。「タイプで打ってあるな。リッツ・ホテルからだ」

「へえ、なんだか変わった名前だなあ」トニーが判事の後ろからのぞきこんで言った。「ユーリック・ノーマン・オーエンか」

「ありがとう、マーストン君。いい指摘をしてくれた」と判事。「さて、そろそろ、招待主について知っていることをすべて話しあうときだと思う。わたしたちはみな、彼の招待客だ。いったい、どんなふうに招かれたのかね？」

ミス・ブレントが最初に話しはじめた。「手紙が届いたんです。2、3年前に会ったという女性からのものでした。でも、差出人の名前が読みづらくてね。オリヴァーか、オグデンだと思ったのですよ。ミセス・オリヴァーも、ミス・オグデンも知っていますからね。ですが、オーエンなんて名前の人はまったく知りません」

ミス・ブレントは手紙をポケットから出して、判事に見せた。

「クレイソーンさんは？」判事はそう言って、若い女性のほうを向いた。

ヴェラは、ミセス・オーエンの秘書として雇われたいきさつを説明した。

「マーストン君はどうかね？」と判事。

"I got a message from a friend of mine, Badger Berkeley. He told me to come here for a good time."

"Armstrong?"

"I was called in to examine Mrs. Owen's health."

"General Macarthur?"

"Got a letter from this Owen fellow, saying a few of my friends were here. He invited me to join them."

"Mr. Lombard?"

Lombard had been wondering if he should tell the group the truth. He decided against it. "Same sort of thing," he said. "Got a letter that mentioned mutual friends."

"Now we come to an interesting point," said Wargrave. "The voice on the recording mentioned all of us by name. One of the names was William Blore. However, there is no one named Blore amongst us. And the name Davis was *not* mentioned. Can you explain that, Mr. Davis?"

"I suppose there's no point in hiding it," he said. "I'm William Blore. I'm not from South Africa—"

"I knew it!" cried Lombard.

■good time 楽しい時、都合のよい時　■same sort of thing 同じようなこと
■amongst 前〈文〉〔集団の〕中にいる（= among）　■there's no point in ～してもし
かたがない、何の意味もない

「友だちのバジャー・バークリーから電報があったんです。ここへ遊びにこいってね」

「アームストロング君は?」

「ミセス・オーエンを診察するために呼ばれました」

「マッカーサー将軍?」

「このオーエンという男から手紙が来たんだ。わしの友人も数人来るからとな。友人たちと過ごすようにと招待された」

「ロンバード君?」

ロンバードは、本当のことを打ち明けるべきかと迷っていた。しかし、やめておこうと決めた。「似たようなもんですよ」と言う。「共通の友だちがいるとかいう手紙が来てね」

「さて、ここで興味深い点がひとつある」ウォーグレイヴは言った。「録音された〈声〉は、われわれ全員を名前で呼んでいた。そのひとつがウィリアム・ブロアだ。ところが、われわれの中にブロアという名の者はいない。そして、デーヴィスという名前は呼ばれなかった。これについて説明してもらえるかな、デーヴィス君?」

「もう隠してもしかたないようですね」彼は言った。「わたしがウィリアム・ブロアですよ。南アフリカ出身ではなく――」

「やっぱり!」ロンバードが声をあげた。

"And I run a detective agency in Plymouth," Blore continued. "I was put on this job by a Mr. Owen. He sent a large payment and instructed me to come here and act like a guest. I was given all your names, and I was to watch you all."

"For what reason?"

"For Mrs. Owen's jewels," said Blore. "But now I don't believe there's any such person."

"I think you're right," said the judge, stroking his lip thoughtfully. "Ulick Norman Owen! In Miss Brent's letter, the first name was written clearly enough to be read: Una Nancy. They're the same initials. Ulick Norman Owen, Una Nancy Owen—each time it is U. N. Owen. Or, by a stretch of the imagination, UNKNOWN!"

"But that's crazy!" cried Vera.

"Yes," said the judge darkly. "It appears our host may be a madman."

■run 動 運営・経営する　■stroke 動〔手で〕～をなでる　■thoughtfully 副 考え込んだようすで　■stretch of the imagination 想像力をふくらませること、こじつけ　■unknown 名 知られていない[未知の]人[もの]　■appear 動〔どうやら〕～らしい、〔～と〕思われる　■madman 名 狂人、血迷った人

「プリムスで探偵事務所を開いてるんです」ブロアは続けた。「オーエン氏からこの仕事を依頼されたんですよ。多額の報酬が送られてきて、ここへ来て客として振る舞うよう指示されましてね。みなさんの名前も知らされましたよ。全員を見張るようにということでした」

　「なんのためかね？」

　「ミセス・オーエンの宝石を守るためです」とブロア。「でもいまは、そんな人物はいないんだと思いますね」

　「なるほど、きみの言うとおりだろう」判事はそう言うと、唇を指で撫でながら考えこんだ。「ユーリック・ノーマン・オーエンか！　ブレントさんの手紙では、ファーストネームはなんとか読める程度に書かれているな。ユーナ・ナンシー。おや、同じ頭文字じゃないか。ユーリック・ノーマン・オーエン、ユーナ・ナンシー・オーエン──どちらも、U・N・Owenだ。少しばかり想像力をふくらませたら、UNKNOWN*になるぞ！」

　「でも、そんなの、気ちがいじみてるわ！」ヴェラが声をあげた。

　「そうだ」判事は暗い声で言った。「われわれの招待主は狂人かもしれんな」

＊UNKNOWN：誰かわからない、未知の人

Chapter Four

The group fell silent.

"I was invited here by an old friend of mine, Lady Constance Culmington," continued the judge. "I have not seen her in many years, but recently I received a letter from her inviting me to meet her here." The judge pulled out the letter from his pocket and put it on the table.

"This brings up an important point," he said. "Whoever invited us all here knows us well, or has worked very hard to find out a good deal about us. He knows, for example, that I am friends with Lady Culmington. He knows Tony Marston's friend Badger and what kind of message he would send. He knows where Miss Brent was two summers ago."

He paused.

"And he has accused us of certain things," he said.

The group began to cry out, defending themselves of the crimes they had been accused of.

■fall silent〔人が急に〕沈黙する、黙り込む　■bring up〔話題・問題などを〕持ち出す、指摘する、提示する　■a good deal いろいろな〜、かなりの〜　■pause 動〔動作を〕休止する、ためらう　■accuse someone of（人）を〜のかどで告発する、〜という理由で（人）を非難する

第4章

　みんなが沈黙して、しんとなった。

　「わたしは、古い友人のレディー・コンスタンス・カルミントンに、ここ
へ招待されたのだ」判事は続けた。「何年も会っていなかったのに、つい最
近、ここで会いたいという手紙を受け取ってね」判事はポケットから手紙
を取りだすと、テーブルの上に置いた。

　「これで重要なことが見えてきたな。われわれを招いた者が誰であれ、そ
の人物はわれわれ全員のことをよく知っている。もしくは、わざわざ細かく
調べ上げているのだ。たとえば、わたしがレディー・カルミントンと友人
だということを知っている。また、トニー・マーストン君の友人バジャー
のことや、彼がどんな電報を送りそうかも知っている。ブレントさんが2年
前の夏に行った場所も知っている」

　彼はいったん口をつぐんだ。

　「そしてわれわれを、それぞれの事件の犯人だと告発しているのだ」

　みんなが口々に声をあげ、告発された罪について自分を弁護しはじめた。

The judge raised his hand, silencing everyone again.

"I am accused of killing an Edward Seton," said the judge. "I remember Seton well. He came before me in court for murdering an old woman. His lawyer defended him well and the jury believed Seton was innocent. However, given the evidence, I knew Seton was guilty. I convinced the jury of his guilt and sentenced him to death. I feel perfectly at peace on the matter. Justice was served."

Then Vera spoke up.

"I'm accused of killing a boy, Cyril. I was his governess. He wasn't allowed to swim far in the sea. One day, when I wasn't paying attention, he started swimming. I went after him, but I couldn't get there in time... It was awful... But it wasn't my fault. The Coroner found me innocent. Even Cyril's mother did not blame me. It wasn't my fault!" She broke into tears.

General Macarthur patted her on the shoulder.

"There, there," he said. "Of course it's not your fault. This whole thing is madness."

Looking at the others, he said firmly, "It's not true what that recording said about Arthur Richmond. Richmond was one of my officers. I sent him on a reconnaissance. He was killed. It's only natural in a war."

■convince 動 説得する、納得させる　■sentence 動〔人に〕判決を言い渡す
■governess 图〔特に住み込みの〕女性家庭教師　■pay attention 注意を払う、気を配る［留める］　■break into tears ワッと泣きだす　■firmly 副 きっぱりと、毅然と
■officer 图 将校　■reconnaissance 图 偵察、予備調査

判事は片手をあげて、ふたたびみんなを黙らせた。

　「わたしはエドワード・シートン殺害の罪で告発されている」判事は言った。「シートンのことはよく覚えているよ。老女殺害の容疑で、わたしの法廷へやってきた。弁護人の弁護が見事だったので、陪審員はシートンが無実だと信じていた。しかし証拠を見れば、シートンが有罪なのは明らかだった。わたしは有罪にするよう陪審員を説得し、死刑の判決を言いわたした。この件について、後ろめたいところはまったくない。正義が果たされたのだよ」

　すると、ヴェラが話しはじめた。

　「わたしがシリルという男の子を殺しただなんて。わたしはシリルの家庭教師だったんです。あの子は海で遠くまで泳ぐことを禁じられていました。でもある日、わたしが目を離したすきに泳ぎだしてしまって。あわてて後を追いましたが、間に合わなかったんです……ああ、なんてひどい……。でも、わたしのせいじゃありません。検視官は無実だと言ってくれたし、シリルのお母さんでさえ、わたしを責めたりしなかったんです。わたしのせいじゃないんです！」彼女はわっと泣きだした。

　マッカーサー将軍がヴェラの肩をやさしくたたいた。

　「まあ、まあ」と言う。「もちろん、あんたのせいじゃない。これはぜんぶ、狂人の仕業だよ」

　そして他の人たちに目を向けると、将軍はきっぱりと言った。「アーサー・リッチモンドの件で、あの録音が言ったことは真実ではないぞ。リッチモンドはわしの部下で、将校のひとりだった。わしは彼を偵察に送った。そして彼は殺された。戦争ではよくあることだ」

"Yes," said Lombard. "A war is a war. About those African men—I admit it, I left them. It was either save myself or save them. We were in the wild. I took what food I could and got out of there."

"You left your men to starve?" asked General Macarthur.

"Like I said, it was either save myself or save them," said Lombard.

Tony Marston spoke up then. "John and Lucy Combes... They must have been the kids I ran over in Cambridge. Terrible luck." Tony picked up his glass and went to the row of bottles on the table to refill it. "It wasn't my fault," he said over his shoulder. "It was just an accident!"

Rogers was next to share his story.

"That recording said my wife and I killed Miss Brady. It's not true. We worked for Miss Brady for many years. She was very ill, and one night there was a storm. The power went out and we couldn't call the doctor. I went out in the storm to get the doctor, but he got there too late. We'd done everything we could for Miss Brady," said Rogers shaking his head.

"I bet you came into a lot of money after she died," said Blore.

■starve 動 飢えに苦しむ、餓死する　■run over〔人・動物などを〕車でひく　■refill 動 ～を補充する、おかわりする　■go out 機能しなくなる　■bet 動 きっと～だと断言する、～に違いない

「そのとおり」ロンバードが言った。「戦争って、そういうもんですよ。あのアフリカの部族民の話だけど——認めますよ、おれが置き去りにしたんです。自分を守るか、あいつらを守るか、そのどちらかだったんでね。荒野に入りこんでしまったから、あるだけ全部の食料を持って逃げたんですよ」

　「部下を見捨てて、飢え死にさせたのか?」マッカーサー将軍が訊いた。

　「さっき言ったじゃないですか。自分を守るか、あいつらを守るかのどちらかだったんだ」

　それから、トニー・マーストンが話しだした。「ジョンならびにルーシー・コームズ……。きっと、ケンブリッジで車でひいた子どもたちだな。運が悪かったんだ」トニーはグラスを取りあげると、酒瓶の並ぶテーブルのところへ行き、酒を注いだ。「ぼくのせいじゃありませんよ」と、肩ごしに言った。「ただの事故だったんだ!」

　つぎはロジャーズが話す番だった。

　「録音では、わたしと妻がブレイディーさまを殺したと言っておりましたね。とんでもないことでございます。わたしたちは長年ブレイディーさまにお仕えしておりました。ブレイディーさまは重いご病気でした。ある夜、嵐になり、電話が通じなくてお医者さまを呼べなかったのです。わたしは嵐の中へ出て、お医者さまを呼びにいきましたが、来てもらったときはもう手遅れでした。わたしたちはブレイディーさまのために、できるかぎりのことをしたのです」と言って、ロジャーズは首を振った。

　「その女主人が死んだあと、きっと、かなりの金が転がりこんだんだろう」とブロアが言った。

"Yes, but we had worked for her for many years," said Rogers. "There's nothing wrong with that."

"What about you?" Lombard challenged Blore.

"Me? I investigated a bank robbery, caught the man, and he went to prison. He happened to die in prison, but that's not my fault," said Blore.

"I remember the Landor case," said Judge Wargrave. "Didn't you get a promotion after putting Landor away?"

"Yes," said Blore quietly.

Suddenly, Lombard laughed. "What a good group of citizens we all are! What about you, doctor? Just a little mistake? A bad operation, right?"

"I have no idea what that recording was talking about. Clees? Close? I can't remember having a patient by that name," said the doctor. But he thought to himself, "I was so drunk…I killed her! The nurse knew, but she never told anyone…Or did she?"

* * *

Everyone was now looking at Emily Brent, but she did not say anything.

"Rogers, is there anyone else on the island?" asked the judge.

"Nobody, sir."

■challenge 動〔人に〕たてつく、異議を申し立てる　■investigate 動〔犯罪や人など を〕捜査する、取り調べる　■robbery 名《法律》強盗（罪）　■promotion 名昇進、昇 格　■operation 名《外科》手術

「ええ、ですが、わたしたちは何年もお仕えしてきたのです」とロジャーズ。「何も悪いことはないはずでございます」

「そう言うあんたは、どうなんだ？」ロンバードがブロアに詰問した。

「わたしですか？　銀行強盗の捜査をしてあの男を逮捕し、そいつが刑務所行きになったんですよ。たまたま刑務所の中で死にましたがね。わたしのせいじゃない」ブロアは言った。

「ランドーの事件なら覚えているよ」ウォーグレイヴ判事が口を挟んだ。「ランドーを刑務所に送ったあと、きみは昇進したのではなかったかね？」

「そうです」ブロアは静かに答えた。

するといきなり、ロンバードが笑いだした。「みんな、なんて善良な市民の集まりなんだ！　さて、あんたはどうですか、先生？　小さな医療ミス？　それとも手術の失敗ですか？」

「あの録音がなんのことを言ってるのか、わたしにはまったくわからないんです。クリースでしたっけ？　クロースだったかな？　そんな名前の患者は思い出せませんね」と医師は言った。しかし、心の中ではこう思っていた。「ひどく酔っていたんだ……わたしが彼女を殺してしまった！　看護婦は知っているが、誰にも話さなかったはずだ……それとも、話したのか？」

＊　＊　＊

いまや全員の目がエミリー・ブレントに注がれていた。しかし、彼女は何も話そうとしなかった。

「ロジャーズ、島には他に誰かいるのかね？」判事が尋ねた。

「いいえ、誰もおりません」

"I am not sure why Unknown has invited us all here, but Unknown may be a dangerous person. I suggest we leave this island right now," said the judge.

"We have no boat, sir," said Rogers. "Fred Narracott comes every morning with the mail and milk, and he takes our orders for supplies."

"Then we should all leave when he comes tomorrow."

Everyone agreed, except for Anthony Marston.

"You want to leave before solving the mystery?" said Marston. "I think it's rather exciting. I say let's stay—might be fun!" With that, he drank down his whiskey. Suddenly, he choked. His face turned purple. He gasped for breath, then slid from his chair, his glass falling from his hand.

■supply 図《suppliesの形で》生活必需品、補給品　■drink down 飲み干す、一気飲みする　■gasp 動苦しそうにあえぐ、息が止まる

「このアンノウンという招待主が、なぜわれわれを招いたのかわからん
が、危険な人物かもしれん。この島をすぐに出たほうがいいだろう」と判
事。

　「それが、ここにはボートがないのでございます」ロジャーズが言った。
「フレッド・ナラコットが毎朝来て手紙と牛乳を届けてくれ、必要なものの
注文を取っていくのです」

　「では、明日彼が来たら、みんなでこの島を去ることにしよう」

　それぞれが賛成の声をあげたが、アンソニー・マーストンだけが反対し
た。

　「謎も解かずに島を出たいんですか？」とマーストン。「ぼくは、わくわ
くするなあ。島にいませんか——おもしろそうですよ！」そう言いながら、
マーストンはウィスキーを飲みほした。だがそのとたん、苦しげにむせは
じめた。顔がみるみる紫色になっていく。息をしようとあえぎながら椅子
からすべりおち、その手からグラスが落ちた。

覚えておきたい英語表現

<u>Sitting</u> in the first-class train car, Judge Lawrence Wargrave smoked his cigar and glanced at his watch. (p. 12, 1行目)

ロレンス・ウォーグレイヴ判事は一等列車の席にすわり、葉巻をくゆらせながら時計に目をやった。

【解説】この文の冒頭のSitting～は、いわゆる「分詞構文」といわれるもので「～しながら」という意味を表します。別名「～ing形の副詞的用法」ともいいます。以下、詳しく見ていきましょう。

◆「分詞」とは？

　英語の文法では、「分詞」には**現在分詞**（動詞のing形）と**過去分詞**（動詞のed形）の2つがあります。現在分詞は「～している」という意味で、過去分詞は「～される」という意味です。

　分詞は、それぞれ「形容詞的に使われるもの」と「副詞的に使われるもの」があります。

◆分詞の形容詞的用法

（1）現在分詞の形容詞的用法：「～している」が基本的な意味

A black dog is **running**. （黒い犬が走っている）

We tried to catch that **running** dog.
（私たちはその走っている犬を捕まえようとした）

Don't wake up the baby **sleeping** in the next room.
（隣の部屋で眠っている赤ちゃんを起こさないでください）

（2）過去分詞の形容詞的用法：「〜される」が基本的な意味

My camera was **stolen** yesterday. （私のカメラが昨日、盗まれた）

The police found my **stolen** camera.
（警察が私の盗まれたカメラを見つけた）

This is a sweater **given** by my mother.
（これは母から贈られたセーターです）

◆分詞の副詞的用法［分詞構文］

（1）現在分詞の副詞的用法

それでは、現在分詞の、「副詞的用法」から見ていきましょう。

まず、分詞構文を使う目的は、長くなりそうな文を、短く、コンパクトにすることによって読者に印象づけるという働きがあります。ですので、紙面が限られた新聞とか、テレビの字幕などでたくさん目にします。

分詞構文を使うのは、一部を省略しても、他の意味に取られない場合のときだけです。省略するのは、カンマでつながっている2つの文のうち、一方の文の「接続詞」と「主語」です。そこで省略したことを示すために、省略した方の文の動詞をing形にします。元の文に手を加えたという印だと考えるといいでしょう。

具体的に例文を見てみてください。

When you turn to the right, you will see the restaurant.
（接続詞）（主語）
（右に曲がると、レストランが見えますよ）

もとの文章には2つの文が含まれています。最初の方の文に接続詞のWhenがあり、それぞれの文は主語がyouで共通しています。

最初の〈接続詞＋主語（When you）〉を省略しても、他の意味に解釈されることはありません。そこで、省略してしまいます。そのとき、省略したということを示すために最初の文の「動詞」をing形にします。そうすると、以下の文が完成します。

→**Turing** to the right, you will see the restaurant.

（2）過去分詞の副詞的用法

次に過去分詞の「分詞構文」について考えてみましょう。

Because it is written in Old English, this book is very difficult.
（接続詞）（主語）

（古英語〈昔の英語〉で書かれているので、この本はとても難しい）

現在分詞の時と同じように、接続詞と主語を省略しても、他に誤解されることはありませんね。省略したということを表すのに、動詞をing形にします。この文では、writtenではなく、isの方をing形にします。

では、全体を書いてみましょう。

→ **Being** written in Old English, this book is very difficult.

まだ、余分なものが残っている感じですっきりしません。実は英語では、冒頭のBeingも省略することができますので、これも省いてしまいましょう。

完成した英文は、以下のようになります。

→ **Written** in Old English, this book is very difficult.
（古英語で書かれているので、この本はとても難しい）

この文も、「（過去）分詞」で始まっているので、「分詞構文」と言えるのです。

他の例文も見てみましょう。過去分詞の前にはBeingが省略されていることに注意してください。

Painted by Picasso, this picture is very expensive.
（ピカソによって描かれたので、この絵はとても高い）

Surrounded by her family, she looked happy.
（家族に囲まれていて、彼女は幸せそうだった）

> When a little group of people **had gathered** at Oakbridge
> station, a driver stepped forward. (p. 32, 1行目)
>
> 数人の人々がオークブリッジ駅に集まったとき、運転手が近づいてきた。

【解説】このhad gatheredは、いわゆる「過去完了」と言われるもので「(過去の
ある時点より前に) 〜していた」という意味を表します。ミステリーに限らず、英
語で物語や小説を読むときは、時間の前後関係が重要となってきます。以下、詳
しく見ていきましょう。

　皆さんは、過去より前の時間をなんというか、聞いたことがありますか?　中
学生の皆さんはまだ学習していません。大人の方は、大昔に学習したはずですが、
忘れてしまった方もいらっしゃるかもしれません。ヒントは「大昔」です。昔より
もはるかに過去のことを「大昔」と言うように、過去の昔のことですから、「大過
去」と言います。読み方は「だいかこ」です。

　時間の系列順に並べると、「大過去→過去→現在→未来」となります。ここは大
切なので、しっかり覚えておいてください。

　大過去は、〈had + 過去分詞〉で表します。そう、中学生の皆さんも、〈have +
過去分詞〉は「現在完了」だとわかる人も少なくないでしょう。haveの過去形の
hadを使うので、「過去完了」というのです。ここで大切なことを一つ追加します。
実は、「大過去 = 過去完了」ということに気づいた人も多いでしょう。

　いくつかの例文を見ていきましょう。

> I **found** that breakfast time **had been** over.
> 　　過去形　　　　　　　　　　　　　　　　過去完了

　私自身、よくあることなのですが、ホテルに泊まって、夜遅くまで起きていて
次の日の朝、起きてみたら、「朝食タイムが終了していた」なんてことを経験した
ことはありませんか?

> found (気がついた)　　　　　　→　過去
> had been over. (終わっていた)　→　過去完了

2つめの例文です。こちらはこの本の36ページの真ん中あたりにある文です。

This **was** what he'**d hoped** for. （p. 36, 9行目）
　　　　過去形　　　　　　過去完了

（これこそが、彼が待ち望んでいたことだった）

wasが過去形だということはすぐわかりますね。whatは、「関係代名詞のwhat」といって、そのあとに〈主語＋動詞〉を続けて「主語が～すること・もの」という意味を表します。

そして重要なのが、he'dの'dです。これはhadの短縮形です。ですから、what he had hoped forがもとの形です。
もう一つ、例文を見てみましょう。

a rich American **had bought** the little island and **built** a large house on it.
　　　　　　　　　過去完了形　　　　　　　　　　　　　　　過去形
（金持ちのアメリカ人がこの小さな島を買って大邸宅を建てた）　　　（p. 12, 5行目）

この文は、大過去→過去形と並んでいるので時間の経過もわかりやすいでしょう。まず島を買い（大過去）、それから家を建てる（過去）。この逆はあり得ません。
　以上の例文からわかるように、「過去完了」は「過去形」とともに使うということを覚えておいてください。普通、過去のある時点を示さないと、大過去（過去完了）は使えないのです。

And Then
There Were None

Part 2

Chapter Five

Dr. Armstrong ran to Marston, who lay on the ground.

"My God!" Armstrong said. "He's dead!"

Everyone stood in shocked silence. It was unbelievable. Strong, healthy young men didn't just die from choking!

Dr. Armstrong sniffed the young man's glass.

"There was something in his drink. I don't know what exactly, but I think it must have been cyanide." He went to the row of bottles and sniffed the whiskey. "It's not in the bottle," he said.

"You mean—he put the stuff in his glass *himself*?" Lombard asked.

"Suicide? That's not possible! He was so alive!" said Vera, very upset.

■unbelievable 形 信じられない（ほどの）　■sniff 動 匂いを嗅ぐ　■cyanide 名《化学》〔青酸カリなどの〕シアン化物　■suicide 名 自殺（すること）　■alive 形 生き生きとして、生存して

第5章

アームストロング医師が、床に倒れたマーストンに駆けよった。

「なんてことだ！」アームストロングは言った。「死んでいる！」

みんなはショックを受けて、呆然と立ちつくした。信じられない。屈強で健康な若者が、ウィスキーにむせたくらいで死ぬはずがない！

アームストロング医師は、マーストンのグラスの匂いをかいだ。

「飲み物に何か入っていたんですね。正確にはわかりませんが、きっと青酸カリだと思います」それから、ならんだ酒瓶のほうへ行き、ウィスキーの匂いをかいでみた。「瓶には入ってないな」と言う。

「つまり——自分でグラスに毒を入れたってことかい？」ロンバードが訊いた。

「自殺ですって？　そんなの、ありえないわ！　あんなにいきいきしてたのに！」ヴェラがひどく動揺して言った。

"Is there any other possibility?" asked Dr. Armstrong.

Everyone slowly shook their heads. None of the bottles had been tampered with. They had all seen Marston pour his own drink. It followed that he must have put the poison in his glass himself.

"But it just doesn't seem right to me. Marston didn't seem like the type of man who would kill himself," said Blore.

"I agree," said Dr. Armstrong.

✳　✳　✳

Later that night, after everyone had gone to bed, Rogers went into the dining room to clean up. As he cleared away the dishes, he noticed the little soldier figures in the middle of the table.

"That's strange," he thought. "I thought there were ten of them."

✳　✳　✳

■tamper with ～に毒を入れる、～に手を加える　■kill oneself 自殺する《（親しみの ない）他人が自殺したことを客観的に述べる表現》　■clear away 〔食後の食器などを〕 片づける

「他にどんな可能性が考えられますか？」アームストロング医師が訊いた。

　誰もがゆっくりと首を振った。毒を仕込まれた瓶は一本もない。しかも、マーストンが自分でウィスキーをついでいるところを、全員が目撃していたのだ。ということは、彼が自分でグラスに毒を入れたのにちがいない。

　「でも、納得がいきませんね。マーストンは自殺するようなタイプには見えませんでしたよ」とブロアが言った。

　「ええ、わたしもそう思います」アームストロングは言った。

＊　＊　＊

　夜が更けて、みなが寝室へ引きあげたあと、ロジャーズは片づけのためにダイニングルームへ入った。皿を片づけていたとき、テーブルのまん中に置かれた小さな兵隊の人形に気がついた。

　「おや、おかしいな」彼は思った。「10個あったはずだが」

＊　＊　＊

General Macarthur turned in his bed. He could not sleep. He kept thinking of Arthur Richmond. He had liked Richmond—he was a fine fellow. But one could not forgive someone for stealing another man's wife. Macarthur had truly loved his wife, Leslie. She was a beautiful young woman, and he had trusted her completely. Of course, he had forgotten that he was old enough to be her father while Richmond was only one year older than her. When he found out about their affair he was shocked and hurt. God, it had hurt! And his cold rage had grown slowly.

Macarthur had sent Richmond to his death. The war was so bad at the time it was nearly impossible to come back alive. Richmond had died out there, and Macarthur wasn't sorry. He had noticed, however, that Armitage, another officer, had started to look at him oddly. Perhaps he suspected, or even guessed the truth.

But it was all so long ago now. Leslie had died from illness soon after Richmond. Macarthur had lived a lonely life since then, avoiding contact with most people. And now, that recording had brought up that old hidden story...

* * *

■forgive 動〔人の罪などを心底から〕許す、容赦する　■affair 名〔短い間の〕不倫、浮気　■rage 名激しい怒り、激情、憤怒　■sorry 形後悔する、すまないと思って、心苦しく思う　■oddly 副奇妙に（も）、変に　■suspect 動～ではないかと疑う〔うすうす感じる〕、～だろうと思う

マッカーサー将軍はベッドの中で寝返りを打った。どうしても眠れない。ずっとアーサー・リッチモンドのことを考えていたのだ。彼はリッチモンドのことを気に入っていた——いい青年だった。だが、人の妻を盗むようなやつを許せるはずがない。マッカーサーは妻のレズリーを心から愛していた。妻は美しくて若い女で、彼はすっかり信じていた。もちろん、自分が父親といっていいほど年配で、リッチモンドは妻よりひとつ年上なだけということなど、忘れていたのだ。ふたりの関係に気づいたときには、ひどくショックを受けて傷ついた。ああ、本当に胸が張り裂けそうだった！　そして、冷酷な怒りがゆっくりと育っていった。

　マッカーサーはリッチモンドを死地へ送りこんだ。当時の戦況は非常に悪く、生きて帰ることはほぼ不可能だった。リッチモンドは戦地で死に、マッカーサーはつゆほども後悔しなかった。しかし、もうひとりの将校のアーミテッジが妙な目つきで見るようになったことに、彼は気づいていた。アーミテッジは疑っていたか、あるいは、真実を察していたのかもしれない。

　だが、もうずっと昔のことだ。レズリーは、リッチモンドが死んでまもなく、病気で亡くなった。自分はその後、ほとんど人とかかわらずに、孤独に暮らしてきたのだ。それがいまになって、あんな録音が昔の秘密を持ちだしてくるとは……。

＊　＊　＊

Vera lay awake in bed, thinking of Hugo, who had disappeared from her life.

"Where are you now?" she wondered.

She remembered Hugo holding her.

"I love you, Vera," he had said. "But I can't ask you to marry me. I have no money. You know, for three months before Cyril was born, I thought I was going to be a rich man. If Cyril had been a girl, I would have inherited all the family money...It's disappointing, but that's life. Besides, Cyril's a good kid."

Vera's thoughts moved to Cyril, that whining little boy. He had been a small and weak child; she suspected he would not even grow to adulthood. And if he didn't? Then Hugo would take over his brother Maurice's estate...Then they would be able to be together...

Vera looked up at the poem in the frame.

"Ten little soldier boys went out to dine;
One choked his little self and then there were Nine."

"It's just like us this evening," she thought with a shiver.

■inherit 動〔財産を〕相続する ■disappointing 形失望[がっかり]させる（ような）
■besides 副それに、その上、また ■whining 形〔人などが〕めそめそ言う ■take
over〔義務や責任など〕を引き継ぐ[受ける] ■estate 名《法律》財産（権）、遺産

Chapter Six

Dr. Armstrong woke up to Rogers shaking him.

"Doctor! Please wake up," Rogers said.

"What is it, Rogers?"

"My wife...I can't get her to wake!" Rogers looked crazy with fear.

Dr. Armstrong quickly dressed and followed Rogers to Mrs. Rogers's room. She was lying peacefully on her side. He went to her and checked her pulse. He turned slowly to Rogers.

"She's gone," he said.

"No!" cried Rogers.

"What was her health like usually?" asked the doctor.

"She had a bit of rheumatism," said Rogers.

"Did she ever take things to make her sleep?" asked the doctor sharply.

"Not that I know of, sir."

■dress 動衣服を着る、支度する ■peacefully 副安らかに、穏やかに、静かに
■pulse 名〔血管の〕脈（拍） ■gone 形〔人が〕死んだ、すでに亡くなっている
■rheumatism 名《病理》リウマチ ■sharply 副〔言い方が〕はっきりと、厳しく

ヴェラはベッドの中で目を覚ましたまま、ヒューゴーのことを考えていた。彼はヴェラの人生から姿を消してしまった。

　「いま、どこにいるの？」ヴェラはぼんやりと考えた。

　ヒューゴーに抱かれていたときのことを思い出す。

　「愛しているよ、ヴェラ」と彼は言った。「でも、結婚してくれとは言えない。このとおり金がないからね。それでも、シリルが生まれるまえの3ヵ月間は、金持ちになれると思ってたんだよ。もしシリルが女の子だったら一家の財産を相続できたから……。がっかりしたけど、それが人生ってもんだな。それに、シリルはいい子だしね」

　ヴェラの思いはシリルへと移った。いつもめそめそした、小さな男の子。体が小さくて弱い子だった。ちゃんと育って大人になれるのかしら、と思ったくらいだ。もし、なれなかったら？　そしたら、ヒューゴーが兄モーリスの財産を相続する……。そして、ふたりはいっしょになれる……。

　ヴェラは額に入った詩を見あげた。

　　「10人の小さな兵隊さんが食事に出かけたよ。
　　 1人がのどをつまらせて、9人になった」

　「今夜のわたしたちにそっくりだわ」ヴェラはそう思い、ぞくっとした。

第6章

　アームストロング医師は、ロジャーズに揺すられて目を覚ましました。

　「先生！　起きてください」ロジャーズが言った。

　「どうしたんだ、ロジャーズ？」

　「妻が……どうしても目を覚まさないのです！」ロジャーズは恐怖のために取り乱しているようだ。

　アームストロング医師はすばやく着替えると、ロジャーズについてミセス・ロジャーズの部屋へ向かった。彼女が横を向いて、安らかに横になっている。アームストロングは近づいて、脈をとった。ゆっくりとロジャーズのほうを見る。

　「亡くなっているよ」と言った。

　「そんな、まさか！」ロジャーズが叫んだ。

　「ふだんの体の具合はどうだったんだい？」医師は訊いた。

　「少しリューマチがありましたが」とロジャーズ。

　「夜よく眠れるように、何か飲んだかい？」と、きつい口調で尋ねる。

　「わたしの知るかぎりでは飲んでいません」

Armstrong went through the drawer in the table by the bed. He did not find anything unusual.

Rogers said, "She didn't have anything last night, sir, except what *you* gave her..."

* * *

At nine o'clock, the group gathered for breakfast. As they ate eggs, bacon, tea, and coffee, Emily Brent asked, "Is the boat coming?"

"Not yet," said Vera, who had been outside with Lombard and Blore. "And it looks like a storm is coming."

Rogers left the dining room, and Miss Brent commented on how pale he looked.

"Please excuse Rogers," said Dr. Armstrong. "He has had to prepare breakfast by himself. There is some sad news. Mrs. Rogers died in her sleep last night."

Words of shock went around the table.

Vera cried out, "How awful! There's been two deaths on this island since we arrived!"

"What was the cause of death?" asked Judge Wargrave.

"It's hard to say," said the doctor. "I can't form any opinions without knowing her general state of health."

■drawer 图引き出し ■unusual 形まれな、普通でない、目立った ■excuse 動許す、容赦する ■by oneself 自分だけで、ひとりで ■go around ～の周りを回る、～に広まる ■form an opinion 意見を立てる[まとめる] ■general 形通例の、全般的な

アームストロングはベッドわきのテーブルの引き出しを調べた。変わったものは何もない。

　ロジャーズが言った。「妻は昨夜、何も飲みませんでした。そのう、先生がくださった薬以外は……」

＊　＊　＊

　9時になると、人々が朝食をとりに集まってきた。卵、ベーコン、紅茶やコーヒーを口に運びながら、エミリー・ブレントが訊いた。「ボートは来ていますか？」

　「いいえ、まだです」ヴェラが言った。彼女はロンバードとブロアといっしょに外に出ていたのだ。「それに、嵐が来そうなんです」

　ロジャーズがダイニングルームを出ていくと、ミス・ブレンドは、ロジャーズの顔色が悪いようだと言った。

　「ロジャーズを許してやってください」とアームストロングが言う。「朝食をひとりで用意しなければならなかったんです。じつは、悲しいお知らせがあります。ミセス・ロジャーズが昨夜、睡眠中に亡くなりました」

　テーブルのあちこちから驚きの声があがった。

　ヴェラが叫んだ。「ああ、こわいわ！　わたしたちが来てから、この島で2人も亡くなったなんて！」

　「死因はなんですかな？」ウォーグレイヴ判事が訊いた。

　「なんとも言えません」医師は言った。「ふだんの健康状態を知らないことには、判断できませんね」

"She looked like such a nervous person. I suppose her heart gave out after the shock last night," said Vera.

"Or perhaps she died of guilt," said Miss Brent.

"What do you mean?" asked Armstrong.

"You all heard last night. She and her husband were accused of killing an old woman. I think it was true and the shock of hearing it spoken out loud broke her," said Miss Brent.

"It's possible," said Armstrong, "if she had a history of a weak heart…"

"It was an act of God," said Miss Brent. "He strikes down sinners!"

"Did she have anything to eat or drink last night after she went to bed?" asked Blore.

"Rogers says she had nothing," said Armstrong.

"Ah, but he *would* say so!" cried Blore.

"Why?"

"You all saw him last night," Blore said. "After his wife fainted he watched her so closely—it was more than just concern for her health. He was afraid she would start talking! Suppose they had murdered that old lady. Suppose his wife's guilt was driving her mad. Well, he can't let her talk and reveal their secret! He probably slipped her something and made sure she would never say a word about it."

■nervous 形 神経質な　■give out 疲れ果てる、作動しなくなる　■speak out loud 大声ではっきり言う　■strike down 打ち倒す　■sinner 名〔道徳・宗教上の〕罪人 ■concern for 〜に対する懸念、〜への関心　■slip 動〔人に物を〕こっそり渡す

「神経過敏な人のようでしたね。昨夜のショックのせいで、心臓が止まったんじゃないかしら」とヴェラ。

　「もしくは、罪悪感のせいで亡くなったのでしょう」ミス・ブレントが言った。

　「どういうことですか？」とアームストロング。

　「みなさんも昨夜聞いたでしょう。あの夫婦は、年よりの女主人を殺したと告発されたのです。それが本当だから、声に出して暴かれるのを聞いて、そのショックで亡くなったのでしょう」とミス・ブレントは言った。

　「ありえますね」とアームストロング。「もし、心臓が弱いという病歴があれば……」

　「神の御業ですよ」とミス・ブレント。「神が罪人を打たれたのです！」

　「彼女は昨夜、寝室へ行ったあとに、何か食べたり飲んだりしませんでしたか？」ブロアが訊いた。

　「ロジャーズは、何も口にしていないと言っていたが」とアームストロング。

　「ああ、でもロジャーズなら、そう言うに決まってますよ！」ブロアが声をあげた。

　「どうして？」

　「みなさん、昨夜の彼のようすを見たでしょう」とブロア。「奥さんが気を失ったあと、ロジャーズは彼女をじっと見つめていた——体を心配しているだけのようには見えませんでしたね。彼女が何かしゃべりだすんじゃないかと怖れてたんですよ！　きっと夫婦でその老婦人を殺したんでしょう。奥さんは罪の意識で頭がおかしくなりそうだった。だから、彼女にしゃべらせて、秘密を漏らすわけにはいかなかったんだ！　たぶん何かを飲ませて、口を封じたんですよ」

There was a pause. Before anybody could speak, the door opened and Rogers came in.

"Is there anything else I can get you?" Rogers asked.

"What time does the boat usually come in the morning?" asked the judge.

"Between eight and nine, sir. It's almost ten now. I don't know what Narracott could be up to this morning," replied Rogers.

"I'm sorry about your wife," said General Macarthur. "The doctor just told us."

Rogers bent his head.

"Thank you, sir," he said.

* * *

Outside, Lombard watched the sea with Blore.

"I don't think the boat's coming at all," said Blore bitterly. "It's all part of our host's plan."

"We're not leaving this island," said a voice behind them.

They turned to see General Macarthur.

"None of us will ever leave... It's the end, you see. The end of everything..." He turned and walked down to the sea.

Blore looked at Lombard.

■be up to ～しようとして、〔ひそかに〕～しようとたくらんで　■bend 動〔物を〕曲げる、傾ける　■bitterly 副〔怒り・失望などの感情が〕激しく、苦々しく　■you see ほら、あのね、おわかりのように

しばらく沈黙が続いた。誰かが話しだすまえに、ドアがあいて、ロジャーズが入ってきた。

　「他にお入り用のものはありますでしょうか？」ロジャーズが訊いた。

　「ボートはいつも朝の何時に来るのかね？」判事が尋ねた。

　「8時から9時のあいだでございます。もうすぐ10時になりますね。ナラコットは今朝はどうしたのでしょうか、どうもわかりかねます」とロジャーズ。

　「奥さんのことは気の毒だったね」マッカーサー将軍が言った。「先生から聞いたところだよ」

　ロジャーズは頭を垂れて、言った。

　「おそれいります」

＊　＊　＊

　戸外で、ロンバードとブロアが海を見つめていた。

　「ボートは来ないと思うね」ブロアが苦々しそうに言った。「すべてが招待主の計画なんだ」

　「わしらがこの島を出ることはないぞ」と、背後から声がした。

　ふたりが振りかえると、そこにマッカーサー将軍がいた。

　「誰ひとり、出ることはない……終わりなのだ。いいかね、何もかも終わるのだよ……」彼は背を向けると、海のほうへ歩いていった。

　ブロアがロンバードに顔を向けた。

"He's gone out of his mind!" he said. "Maybe we'll all go crazy before this ends!"

* * *

Dr. Armstrong was just about to go out outside when Rogers came to him looking upset.

"Excuse me, doctor, can you come with me?" Rogers said. "In here, sir."

Rogers opened the door to the dining room.

"The little figures," he said as he pointed at the soldiers on the dining room table. "I don't understand. I swear there were ten of them before."

"Yes, ten," said Dr. Armstrong. "We counted them last night at dinner."

"You see, last night when I was cleaning up after dinner, there were nine," said Rogers. "I noticed it and thought it was strange. Now, this morning, there's only eight!"

■go out of one's mind 頭がおかしくなる、正気を失う　■be just about to ～するところだ

「頭がおかしくなったんだ！」と言う。「これが片づくまでに、みんな気が変になってしまうかもしれないぞ！」

＊　＊　＊

アームストロング医師が外に出ようとしたとき、ロジャーズがうろたえたようすで近づいてきた。

「おそれいりますが、先生、いっしょに来ていただけませんでしょうか？」と言う。「こちらでございます」

ロジャーズはダイニングルームのドアをあけた。

「あの小さな人形です」彼はダイニングテーブルの上の兵隊たちを指さした。「わけがわからないのです。まえは、たしかに10個ございました」

「そうだ、10個だよ」とアームストロング。「昨夜、夕食のときに数えたからね」

「それがですね、昨夜夕食の片づけをしたときは、9つしかなかったのです」とロジャーズは言う。「そのことに気づいて、妙だと思っておりました。でもいま見たら、今朝は8つしかないのですよ！」

Chapter Seven

Some time after breakfast, Vera Claythorne and Emily Brent went to the shore to look for the boat. They talked as they walked.

"Miss Brent, do you think it's true that Mr. and Mrs. Rogers killed that old woman?"

"Everything points to it," said Miss Brent. "When they were accused the woman fainted and the man dropped the coffee. Yes, I'm sure it's true."

"But, there were other accusations," said Vera, "against all of us. If it's true about Mr. and Mrs. Rogers, it can't mean that it's true of . . . of us all?"

"Well, Mr. Lombard openly admitted that he left those twenty men. And Judge Wargrave was just doing his job, as was Mr. Blore," said Miss Brent. "I was too, in a sense."

"Oh?" said Vera with interest.

■shore 图 海岸、陸地　■point 動〔事実・結論などを〕強く示唆する　■accusation 图《法律》告発、告訴　■in a sense ある意味では、一面では　■with interest 興味を持って

第7章

　朝食後しばらくして、ヴェラ・クレイソーンとエミリー・ブレントは海岸へ、ボートが来るかどうか見にいった。

　ふたりは歩きながら話していた。

　「ブレントさん、ロジャーズ夫婦が老婦人を殺したのは本当だと、そう思っていらっしゃるんですか？」

　「何もかもがそう示していますよ」ミス・ブレントが言った。「ふたりが告発されたとき、奥さんは気を失ったし、ロジャーズはコーヒーを落としたじゃないの。ええ、まちがいなく本当の話ですよ」

　「でも、他の告発もあったわ」とヴェラ。「わたしたち全員に対しての告発です。ロジャーズ夫婦の件が本当だからって、みんなについても本当だということには……なりませんよね？」

　「そうねえ、ロンバードさんは例の20人を置き去りにしたと、はっきり認めましたね。それから、ウォーグレイヴ判事はご自分の仕事をしただけです。ブロアさんもそうでしょう」ミス・ブレントは言った。「ある意味で、わたしも同じですよ」

　「まあ、そうなんですか？」ヴェラは興味を抱いた。

"Yes. I didn't say anything last night because I didn't think it a decent thing to discuss in front of gentlemen," said Miss Brent. "Beatrice Taylor worked for me. She had good manners, was clean, and was willing to work. But she had loose morals. She went out with men, you know, and one day I found out she was expecting a baby. She wasn't married! Well, I couldn't have that kind of thing in my house. I fired her immediately."

"What happened to her?"

"She killed herself."

"Oh!" cried Vera. "Did you blame yourself?"

"I? I had nothing to do with it. Her own sin drove her to suicide. If she had behaved like a decent woman, none of it would have happened." She looked at Vera with hard, cold eyes, and Vera felt herself trembling.

* * *

Dr. Armstrong walked outside. Philip Lombard stood at the edge of the cliff. Armstrong strongly wanted to talk with someone—he needed to sort out his thoughts.

"Lombard, can I have a word with you?" Armstrong asked.

The two men walked to the shore as they talked.

"There's something funny going on here," Armstrong said. He described what Rogers had found in the dining room.

■**decent** 形〔言動などが倫理的で〕礼儀にかなった、品行正しい　■**be willing to** 進んで〜する、〜に前向きである　■**loose** 形〔人が性的に〕だらしない、〔締めていた物が〕緩んだ　■**fire** 動〈話〉〔従業員・使用人を〕解雇する　■**tremble** 動〔恐怖・怒りなどで〕身震いする　■**at the edge of** 〜のふち[端]に[で]　■**sort out** 整理する、気持ちを落ち着ける　■**have a word with** 〔相談・質問などのために〕（人）と少し話をする

「ええ。昨夜何も言わなかったのは、男の人たちのまえでは話しにくいことだったからです」とミス・ブレント。「ビアトリス・テイラーはわたしの使用人でした。行儀がよくて、きれい好きで、よく働きました。ところが、じつはふしだらな娘だったんですよ。男たちとつき合ったりしてね、ある日、妊娠していることがわかったんです。結婚もしていないのに！ とにかく、わたしの家でそんなことを許すわけにはいきません。その場でくびにしましたよ」

「それで、その娘さんはどうなったんですか？」

「自殺しました」

「まあ！」ヴェラは声をあげた。「ご自分を責めませんでしたか？」

「わたしが？ わたしはなんの関係もありませんよ。あの娘の罪が、自らを自殺へと追いやったのです。きちんとした女性として振る舞っていれば、あんなことにはならなかったんですよ」そう言って、厳しく冷たい目でヴェラを見つめた。ヴェラは思わず身震いした。

＊　＊　＊

アームストロング医師は外を歩いていた。ふと見ると、フィリップ・ロンバードが崖のふちに立っている。アームストロングは誰かと話したくてたまらなかった——頭の中を整理する必要があったのだ。

「ロンバード君、ちょっと話していいかい？」アームストロングは声をかけた。

ふたりは海岸のほうへ歩きながら話した。

「じつは妙なことが起こっているんだ」アームストロングは言った。そして、ロジャーズがダイニングルームで見つけたことを詳しく話した。

"Yes, there were ten at dinner last night," Lombard agreed. "Now there are eight?"

Armstrong recited:

"Ten little soldier boys went out to dine;
One choked his little self and then there were Nine.

Nine little soldier boys sat up very late;
One overslept himself and then there were Eight."

"Fits too well to be a coincidence!" said Lombard. "Marston choked and died, and Mrs. Rogers never woke up!"

"Therefore?" asked Armstrong.

"Therefore, there must be another kind of soldier here—the Unknown Soldier! U. N. Owen! One total lunatic at large!"

"I agree," said Armstrong. "But Rogers said there is no one else on the island, and I don't think he's lying. He's truly scared. He doesn't know what's going on."

"Let's search the island," said Lombard. "It's a bare rock. There can't be many places for a person to hide."

"Yes," said Armstrong, "and let's ask Blore to help us. We three should be able to do this job right."

■recite 動暗唱する、復唱する　■coincidence 名〔偶然の〕一致、合致　■therefore 副 〔前に述べたことの〕結果、だから　■lunatic 形気の狂った、狂気の　■at large 全体として　■bare 形覆いがない、むき出しになった

「そうだな、昨夜の夕食のときには10個あったぞ」とロンバード。「いまは8つだって？」

　アームストロングは詩を暗唱した。

　　「『10人の小さな兵隊さんが食事に出かけたよ。
　　1人がのどをつまらせて、9人になった。

　　9人の小さな兵隊さんが夜ふかしをしたよ。
　　ひとりが寝すごして、8人になった』」

　「偶然にしては、できすぎだな！」ロンバードが言った。「マーストンはのどを詰まらせて死んだし、ロジャーズの女房は目を覚まさなかった！」
　「だから？」とアームストロング。
　「だから、ここには、ちがう兵隊がいるのさ──アンノウンという謎の兵隊がね！　U・N・オーエンだ！　完全に狂ってるんだ！」
　「わたしもそう思うよ」とアームストロング。「だが、ロジャーズは島には他に誰もいないと言っていたし、うそをついているとは思えない。ずいぶんおびえているからね。何が起きてるのかわからないようだ」
　「島を捜索してみようぜ」とロンバード。「ここは裸の岩だ。人が隠れる場所なんてかぎられてるさ」
　「そうだな」アームストロングは言った。「ブロア君にも手を貸してもらおう。3人いれば、うまくいくだろう」

Chapter Eight

Once Lombard and Armstrong explained about the soldiers, Blore agreed to help search the island.

"I wish we had a gun," said Blore. "It'd be good for protection now."

"I have one," said Lombard, patting his pocket.

The other men stared. This new information surprised and worried them. However, they had no choice but to search the island for the madman who was killing off their party.

The task was very simple. It was a small island, and they searched every rock and shadow that looked like it could be the opening of a cave. But there were no caves, and no place where a person could hide. At one point, they came across General Macarthur sitting by the sea.

"Nice spot you found for yourself, sir," said Blore.

■stare 動 じっと見る、凝視する　■have no choice but to ～する以外に選択肢がない、～するしかない　■kill off 皆殺しにする、全滅させる　■cave 名 洞窟《開口部が地上にあるもの》　■come across ～に出くわす、～に遭遇する

第8章

　ロンバードとアームストロングが兵隊の人形のことを説明すると、ブロアも島の捜索に賛成し、手伝うと言った。

　「ピストルを持ってくればよかったな」とブロア。「こういうとき、身を守るのにいいんだが」

　「おれは持ってるよ」ロンバートがそう言って、ポケットを軽くたたいた。

　他のふたりが目を丸くしてロンバードを見つめた。ピストルを持っていると初めて知って、驚くと同時に不安を感じたのだ。しかし、他に選択肢はない。島を捜索して、彼らを皆殺しにしようとしている狂人を見つけだすしかなかった。

　作業はじつに単純だった。小さな島なので、あらゆる岩や、洞窟の入り口のように見える陰を調べた。ところが、洞窟も、人が隠れられるところも見つからない。その途中、マッカーサー将軍が海のそばにすわっているのに出くわした。

　「いい場所を見つけましたね」ブロアが声をかけた。

General Macarthur turned around, surprised that someone was there with him. He had a strange look in his eye.

"Go away. This is the end, but you don't understand that at all. We're never leaving," Macarthur said, almost to himself. Then he turned back to the sea.

"He's crazy," said Blore as they walked off. The thought made them all uncomfortable.

*　*　*

Soon they were finished, and they had found nothing. The three men stood at the edge of the cliff, looking at the sea. Dark clouds were gathering in the sky, and the wind was rising. A storm was coming.

There was only one place on the island left to look: the face of the cliff itself. They would have to lower a man down by rope to look for holes or caves. Lombard said he would do it, and Blore went off to find some rope.

After about twenty minutes, Blore returned with enough rope to lower Lombard down the cliff. Blore and Armstrong stayed at the top and held onto the rope.

■turn around 振り返る、後ろを向く　■walk off 立ち去る　■uncomfortable 形〔物や状況などが〕心地よくない、〔人が〕気詰まりな　■face 名〔崖の〕切り立った面　■hold onto ～をしっかりつかまえておく

マッカーサーが振りかえり、人がいることに驚いた。目つきがおかしい。

　「あっちへ行ってくれ。これは終わりなのだ。だが、きみらにはわからん
だろう。わしらはけっして、ここから出られない」と、彼はひとり言のよ
うに言った。そして海のほうへ向きなおった。
　「頭がおかしくなったようだな」そこを離れながらブロアが言い、その考
えに3人とも気が滅入った。

＊　＊　＊

　やがて島を回りおえたが、何も見つからなかった。3人は崖のふちに立っ
て海を眺めた。空には暗い雲が集まり、風が出てきている。嵐が近づいて
いるのだ。

　島の中で探すところがあと一か所だけ残っている。崖の前面の絶壁だ。誰
かをロープで降ろして、穴や洞窟がないか調べなければならない。ロンバー
ドが、自分がやろうと申し出たので、ブロアがロープを探しにいった。

　20分ほどして、ブロアが戻ってきた。ロンバードを崖に降ろせるくらい
の長さのロープを手にしている。ブロアとアームストロングは崖の上に残
り、ロープをしっかりつかんだ。

"I don't like it," said Armstrong. "I'm not a doctor of mental illnesses, but it's clear General Macarthur has gone out of his mind. We're looking for a *madman*, aren't we?" There was fear in Armstrong's voice.

"Well, I don't like that Lombard has a gun," replied Blore. "Did you bring a gun along with you, Armstrong?"

"No, certainly not!"

"Neither did I," said Blore. "And neither would any other normal person. *So why would Lombard?*"

Just then, there was a sharp pull on the rope. It was Lombard, signaling to be brought up. The men starting pulling, and soon, Lombard was standing with them again.

"There's nothing," Lombard said, wiping the sweat from his face. "He must be hiding in the house."

The three men measured every room and closet in the house to find that there was no space left unaccounted for. There were no false walls or secret hiding places.

As they finished, the three gave each other troubled looks. There was no one on the island but their eight selves.

■certainly not　とんでもない　■signal　動 合図する、信号を送る　■wipe　動〔汚れなどを〕拭く、ぬぐう　■unaccounted for　使途不明の、説明されていない　■give someone a troubled look　（人）に困惑した[心配そうな]顔つきをする[見せる]

「どうも気に入らないな」とアームストロング。「わたしは精神科の医師じゃないが、マッカーサー将軍の頭がおかしくなったのはまちがいない。わたしたちは、たしか狂人を探してるんじゃないのかい？」アームストロングの声に恐怖がにじんでいる。

　「そうだなあ、わたしは、ロンバードがピストルを持ってるのが気に入らないな」ブロアが答えた。「あなたはピストルを持ってきましたか、アームストロング先生？」

　「いいや、持ってくるわけないだろう！」

　「わたしもですよ」とブロア。「ふつうの人はピストルを持ってきたりしない。じゃあ、いったいなぜロンバードは持ってきたんだろう？」

　そのとき、ロープが強く引かれた。ロンバードが、引き上げてくれと合図してきたのだ。ふたりはロープを引っぱりはじめた。しばらくすると、ロンバードは彼らといっしょに崖の上に立った。

　「何もないぜ」ロンバードは顔の汗をぬぐいながら言った。「やつはきっと家の中に隠れてるんだ」

　3人は邸宅内のあらゆる部屋とクローゼットを測ってみた。だが、何に使うかわからないような空間は見つからなかった。

　捜索が終わると、3人は困惑したように顔を見合わせた。彼らの8人以外、島には誰もいないのだ。

Chapter Nine

At noon, Rogers came out onto the terrace to call everybody to lunch. When everybody had gathered in the dining room, they realized General Macarthur had not come.

"I was taking a walk earlier and I saw him," said Vera. "He was just sitting on the beach. He probably didn't hear the call to lunch."

"I'll go get him," said Dr. Armstrong. "You should all start eating."

Lunch consisted entirely of things out of cans, since there was no longer a cook. The group tried to make small talk, but it proved difficult. As Rogers went around collecting everybody's plates, he suddenly stopped.

"There's somebody running..." he said, staring out the window. Then they all heard the rapid footsteps, and Dr. Armstrong came bursting through the door.

"General Macarthur—" he paused, as if not believing what he was about to say. "He's dead!"

■earlier 副〔時間的に〕前に ■consist of ～から成る、～で構成される ■entirely 副 もっぱら、ひたすら ■no longer もはや～でない ■burst through ～を突き破って 進む

第9章

　正午にロジャーズがテラスへ出てきて、昼食の用意ができたと知らせた。みんながダイニングルームに集まったとき、マッカーサー将軍が来ないことに気がついた。

　「さっき散歩のとちゅうでお会いしたわ」ヴェラが言った。「浜辺にすわっておられたから、たぶん昼食の知らせが聞こえなかったんでしょう」

　「わたしが呼んできますよ」とアームストロング。「先に始めてください」

　昼食は缶詰から出したものばかりだった。もう料理人がいないからだ。食べながら世間話でもしようとしてみたが、ぎこちなくなるだけだった。ロジャーズは客たちの皿を集めてまわりだしたが、突然、手を止めた。

　「誰かが走ってきます……」と、窓の外を見つめて言った。すると、慌ただしい足音が聞こえ、アームストロング医師がドアを勢いよくあけて飛びこんできた。
　「マッカーサー将軍が──」と言いよどんだ。自分が言おうとしていることが信じられないかのように。「亡くなった！」

Seven people looked at each other and could find no words to say.

*　*　*

The storm hit just as General Macarthur's body was being brought into the house. As Blore and Armstrong carried the body upstairs, Vera was taken hold of by a strange feeling. She suddenly went into the dining room and looked at the table. She stood there, unable to move for a moment or two. Then Rogers entered the room.

"Oh, Miss, I just came to see..." he started, then broke off.

"Yes, Rogers. You're right," she said. *There are only seven.*

*　*　*

After the general was laid in his bed and Armstrong finished his examination, he joined the others in the drawing room. Miss Brent was knitting. Vera stood by a window, looking out at the storm. Blore and Wargrave sat in large chairs, and Lombard was walking nervously up and down.

"Well, doctor?" asked Wargrave.

Armstrong was shaking, but he tried to control himself.

"There's no question about it," he said. "Macarthur was hit in the back of the head with a hard object."

■take hold of 牛耳る、制する　■break off 途中でやめる、中止する　■lay 動~を横たえる[寝かせる]　■knit 動編み物をする　■stand by そばに立つ[いる]

7人は言葉を失い、たがいに顔を見合わせた。

＊　＊　＊

　マッカーサー将軍の遺体が家に運びこまれたのと同時に、嵐がやってき
た。ブロアとアームストロングが遺体を2階へ抱えていくのを見ているうち
に、ヴェラは嫌な予感に襲われた。いきなりダイニングルームへ駆けこみ、
テーブルを見つめる。そこに立ったまま、しばらく動けなかった。やがて
ロジャーズが入ってきた。
　「ああ、クレイソーンさま、わたしも見にきたところで……」と言いかけ
て、口をつぐんだ。
　「そうよ、ロジャーズ。あなたの思っているとおりよ」ヴェラは言った。
「人形は7つしかないわ」

＊　＊　＊

　将軍をベッドに横たえて、遺体のようすを調べたあと、アームストロング
は客間にいるみんなのところへ行った。ミス・ブレントが編み物をしてい
た。ヴェラは窓のそばに立ち、外の嵐のようすを見ている。ブロアとウォー
グレイヴは長椅子にすわり、ロンバードはいらいらと歩きまわっている。

　「どうかね、先生？」ウォーグレイヴが訊いた。
　アームストロングは体が震えていたが、なんとか落ち着こうとした。
　「間違いありませんね」と言う。「マッカーサー将軍は後頭部を硬いもの
で殴られたんです」

There was shocked silence. Wargrave was the first to speak again. He took control of the situation as someone who had long been used to being an authority figure.

"So we know," he said, "that this was a murder."

Everyone looked at each other with fearful eyes.

"As I sat on the terrace this morning, I saw you three gentlemen walking around the island," said Judge Wargrave. "I assume you were searching for Mr. Owen?"

"Yes, sir," said Lombard. "We found no one. There can't be anybody hiding on this island—it's simply not possible."

"Then that brings us to the logical if unpleasant conclusion," said the judge. *"One of us must be U. N. Owen!"*

"Oh, no!" cried Vera. Judge Wargrave turned his eyes on her.

"My dear, we must look at the facts," he said. "We are all in danger. One of us is U. N. Owen, but we do not know which of us. Of the ten people who came to the island, three have been cleared of guilt: Tony Marston, Mrs. Rogers, and General Macarthur. There are seven of us left, and one of us must be Mr. or Miss Unknown. Do you all agree?"

"I suppose you're right," said Armstrong.

"We must look at the evidence. Does anybody have something to say that might be helpful?"

■authority figure 権威のある人 ■turn one's eyes on ～に[の方へ]目[視線]を向ける ■in danger 危機に直面している ■clear 動〔人の〕疑いを晴らす

みんなはショックを受けて、黙りこんだ。最初にふたたび口を開いたのは
ウォーグレイヴだった。権威を持つことに長年慣れてきた者として、ウォー
グレイヴはその場の指揮を執った。

　「では、これは殺人だとわかったわけだ」彼は言った。

　全員がおびえた目で、たがいに視線を交わした。

　「今朝テラスにすわっているあいだ、きみたち3人が島を歩きまわるのを
見ていたよ」とウォーグレイヴ判事。「オーエンを探していたのではないか
ね？」

　「ええ、そうですよ」ロンバードが言った。「でも見つかりませんでした。
この島には誰も隠れているはずがない──とにかく不可能なんだ」

　「そうすると、不愉快ではあるが論理的に次のような結論が出る」判事は
言った。「われわれの中のひとりが、U・N・オーエンにちがいない！」

　「そんな、まさか！」ヴェラが声をあげた。ウォーグレイヴ判事は彼女に
目を向けた。

　「お嬢さん、事実を直視せねばならんのだよ」と言う。「みんなが危険に
さらされている。われわれの中のひとりがU・N・オーエンなのに、それ
が誰かわからないのだ。島に来た10人のうち、3人はすでに嫌疑が晴れて
いる。トニー・マーストン、ミセス・ロジャーズ、そしてマッカーサー将
軍だ。残りはわれわれ7人、その中のひとりがミスター・アンノウンか、ミ
ス・アンノウンにちがいない。みんな、賛成してもらえるかね？」

　「おっしゃるとおりだと思いますよ」アームストロングが言った。

　「では、証拠を調べねばならんな。誰か、役に立ちそうな証言はあるか
ね？」

"Lombard has a gun!" burst out Blore.

Smiling coldly, Lombard decided to tell the truth of how he had been invited to the island. He told them of Mr. Morris, and how he had been instructed to bring a gun.

"But what proof do you have?" Blore asked Lombard. "There's no way we can make sure your story is true!"

"We cannot prove anybody's story," cut in Judge Wargrave. "We must look at each death and see if there is anybody we can say is innocent with absolute certainty. Now, with Marston, I don't think there's anything we can say. Any one of us could have slipped something in his drink without being noticed. But with Mrs. Rogers—perhaps we can get somewhere with that. Last night, after we all heard the recording, Mrs. Rogers fainted. We all left the drawing room to look at the record player, except for Rogers, who went to get brandy, and Miss Brent, who stayed in the room with Mrs. Rogers. When we returned to the drawing room, Miss Brent was leaning over Mrs. Rogers."

Miss Brent, who had sat calmly all this time, turned bright red.

"I was helping the poor woman!" she cried out.

■There's no way ~ 〜ということなどあり得ない[とてもできない]　■make sure〔事実・行動などに間違いがないかを〕確かめる　■cut in 割り込む、話を遮る　■see if 〜 かどうかを確かめる　■say with absolute certainty 断言する、絶対的な確信を持って 〜を言う　■lean over 〜に身を乗り出す

「ロンバード君はピストルを持っています！」ブロアがいきなり大声を出した。

ロンバードは冷たい微笑を浮かべると、島へ招待された経緯について、本当のことを話しだした。モリスのことや、ピストルを持っていくよう命じられたことも語った。

「でも、どんな証拠があるんだ？」ブロアがロンバードに尋ねた。「きみの話が本当だと確かめる方法などないぞ！」

「誰の話も証明などできんよ」ウォーグレイヴ判事がさえぎった。「ひとつひとつの死について、たしかに無実だと言える者がいるかどうか、それを調べねばならんのだ。さて、マーストン君についてだが、言えることは何もないだろう。われわれの中の誰もが、気づかれずに彼の飲み物に何かを入れることができたからね。だが、ミセス・ロジャーズについては──いくらか言えることがありそうだ。昨夜、例の録音を聞いたあと、ミセス・ロジャーズは気を失った。それから、みんなはレコードプレーヤーを見に隣室へ行った。ブランデーを取りにいったロジャーズと、客間で彼女のそばにいたブレントさんを除いてね。われわれが客間に戻ると、ブレントさんは彼女の上に身をかがめていた」

いままでずっと静かにすわっていたミス・ブレントが、顔を真っ赤にした。

「わたしは哀れな女性を介抱していたのですよ！」と、声を荒げた。

"I am just stating the facts," said Wargrave. "Then Rogers came in with the brandy, which he could have poisoned before he entered the room. Mrs. Rogers drank the brandy, and shortly afterward she was led to her bedroom by Dr. Armstrong and Mr. Rogers."

"Yes! That's right! So that rules out me, Mr. Lombard, Judge Wargrave, and Miss Claythorne," said Blore.

"Does it?" asked the judge. "We must think of *every* possibility. It is very possible that any one of us could have gone up to her room later and given her something. The doctor gave her sleeping medicine. She would have been sleepy and confused—any of us could have given her something without too much of a fight."

"But Rogers would have been there—it's his room too!" said Blore.

"No, Rogers was downstairs, cleaning up after dinner," said the judge. "So we have established the fact that no one can really be cleared of guilt. Now, as for General Macarthur. That happened this morning. I was sitting on the terrace all morning, but of course there were plenty of moments where I suppose I could have gone after Macarthur without anybody noticing. Miss Brent, how about you?"

■poison 動~に毒を盛る　■shortly afterward それから間もなく　■rule out 除外する、排除する　■establish the fact that ～という事実を立証する　■as for ～はどうかと言うと

「事実を述べているにすぎんよ」とウォーグレイヴ。「それからロジャーズがブランデーを持って入ってきた。そのブランデーに、部屋に入るまえに毒を盛ることもできただろう。彼女はブランデーを飲み、しばらくして、アームストロング先生とロジャーズに連れられて寝室へ行った」

「そうですよ！　そのとおりです！　だから、わたしとロンバード君、ウォーグレイヴ判事、それにクレイソーンさんは除外されますね」ブロアが言った。

「そうかね？」判事が尋ねた。「あらゆる可能性を考えねばならん。われわれのひとりがあとから彼女の部屋へ行って、何かを飲ませたということも十分ありえる。先生が睡眠薬を与えたから、彼女は眠くてぼんやりしていたはずだ——たいして抵抗されずに、誰でも飲ますことができただろう」

「でも、ロジャーズがいたでしょう——彼の部屋でもあるんだから！」とブロア。

「いや、ロジャーズは一階で夕食の後片づけをしていた」判事は言った。「つまり、全員必ずしも潔白ではないという事実が立証されたわけだ。さて、次にマッカーサー将軍の件を見てみようか。これが起こったのは今朝のことだ。わたしは午前中ずっとテラスにすわっていた。だがもちろん、誰にも気づかれずにマッカーサー将軍のあとを追いかけようと思えば、その時間はたっぷりあっただろう。ブレントさん、あなたはどうですかな？」

"I was knitting on the terrace all morning," she replied.

"I did not see you there," said the judge.

"No, I was around the corner, out of the sun."

"So you could have killed Macarthur without anybody noticing either."

Miss Brent said nothing.

"I was with Lombard and Armstrong all morning," cut in Blore.

"But you went back to the house for a rope," said Armstrong. "And Lombard went off by himself for a few minutes too!"

"I was testing an idea I had!" said Lombard. "I thought I might be able to use a mirror to send light signals to the village. It didn't work, though..."

"So you three were all alone at some point in the morning?" the judge asked.

After a pause, one of them replied, "Yes."

The judge then turned to Vera, saying, "How about you?"

"I took a walk around the beach. I saw General Macarthur and spoke to him a little. But he seemed... strange," she said. "He was talking about how this is the end. It didn't make sense, so I came back to the house."

■around the corner 角を曲がったところに　■go off by oneself 単独行動を取る、ひとりになる　■at some point いつか、ある時点で　■after a pause 〔話の途中で〕一瞬の間を置いて　■make sense 意味をなす、道理にかなう

「午前中はずっとテラスで編み物をしていましたよ」ミス・ブレントが答えた。

「テラスであなたを見かけなかったがね」と判事。

「ええ、わたしは角をまがったところにいたんです。日が当たらないようにね」

「では、あなたも、誰にも気づかれずにマッカーサー将軍を殺せたわけだ」

ミス・ブレントは何も言おうとしない。

「わたしは午前中ずっと、ロンバード君とアームストロング先生といっしょにいましたよ」ブロアが割って入った。

「でも、きみはロープを取りに家へ戻ったじゃないか」とアームストロングが言った。「それに、ロンバード君も数分間ひとりでどこかへ行ってただろう！」

「ちょっといいことを思いついたから、試してたのさ！」とロンバード。「鏡を使ったら、村に光で合図を送れるかもしれないって思ってね。まあ、うまくいかなかったが……」

「それでは、3人とも午前中にひとりでいたときがあったわけだね？」判事が訊いた。

一瞬の間をおいて、3人のうちのひとりが答えた。「そのとおりです」

判事は次にヴェラに向かって言った。「きみはどうかね？」

「浜辺で散歩をしていました。マッカーサー将軍に出会ったので、少しお話しました。でも、あの人はなんだか……ようすが変だったわ」とヴェラ。「これで終わりだ、というようなことを言っていたけれど、なんのことかわからなくて、それで家に戻ってきたんです」

"Finally, there's Rogers," said the judge. They called Rogers into the room and he explained that he had been busy all morning, cleaning up breakfast and preparing lunch. He also said he saw eight soldier figures on the table before lunch.

After a thoughtful pause, the judge spoke again.

"Ladies and gentlemen, after going over the facts, we have established that any one of us could be the killer. Nobody has a good alibi for any of the deaths. All we can do at this time is to try to contact the village for help." After a pause, the judge added, "I believe we are in great danger. I suggest that everyone be very careful—the killer is among us."

*   *   *

The group spent the rest of the afternoon inside, hoping that the rain would stop. Vera and Lombard walked through the house. Miss Brent went to her room to write in her journal, Rogers made himself busy in the kitchen, and Armstrong and Wargrave spent time talking in the drawing room. At tea time, they all gathered again in the drawing room and shared an uncomfortable silence.

■go over〔詳細に〕～を調べる　■alibi 図アリバイ、現場不在証明　■walk through ～を通って歩く　■write in one's journal 日記をつける

「最後に、ロジャーズの話を聞こうか」判事が言った。ロジャーズを部屋に呼ぶと、彼は午前中、朝食の片づけと昼食の用意に追われていたと答えた。また、昼食前にはテーブルに兵隊の人形が8つあったことも話した。

しばらく考えたあと、判事はまた話しだした。

「みなさん、事実を調べた結果、われわれのうち誰もが犯人であり得るということが立証された。どの殺人についても、完全なアリバイを持つ者はいないからね。いまできることは、なんとか村に連絡して助けを呼ぶことだけだろう」少し黙ってから、こうつけ加えた。「われわれは非常に危険な状況にある。みんな十分気をつけるように——われわれの中に殺人者がいるのだから」

＊　＊　＊

人々は雨がやむのを待ちわびながら、その日の午後を屋内で過ごした。ヴェラとロンバードはいっしょに家の中を歩いていた。ミス・ブレントは部屋にこもって日記をつけ、ロジャーズは台所で忙しく働き、アームストロングとウォーグレイヴは客間で世間話をして時間をつぶした。お茶の時間には、全員がふたたび客間に集まったが、おたがい気まずく黙りこんでいた。

When Rogers brought in the tea, closed the curtains, and turned on the lamps, the room was filled with light and the group started to feel better. Rogers went back out and the guests settled in for tea. They tried to act as if everything was all right.

"I've lost two balls of yarn," said Miss Brent, knitting. "It's very strange."

Suddenly, Rogers came into the room.

"Excuse me, but does anyone know what's happened to the bathroom curtain?" he asked. "It's gone! The red curtain that hung in the bathroom on the first floor—it's disappeared!"

"Was it there this morning?" asked the judge.

"Yes, sir."

"What does it matter?" asked Blore. "You can't kill anybody with a red curtain."

"Yes, sir," said Rogers. He turned to leave, but he was trembling. The group went back to their tea, but they all eyed each other with concern.

■be filled with ～で満たされている、～でいっぱいである　■feel better 気が楽になる、気が晴れる　■settle in〔新しい環境に慣れて〕落ち着く　■yarn 図〔編み物・織り物に用いる〕糸　■What does it matter? それがどうしたというの？　■with concern 心配して

お茶を持ってきたロジャーズがカーテンを閉めてランプを灯すと、部屋が明るくなったせいか、みんなの気持ちもいくらか軽くなってきた。ロジャーズが台所へ戻ると、客たちは席に着いてお茶を飲み、何事もないかのように振る舞おうとした。

　「毛糸の玉がふたつなくなったんですよ」ミス・ブレントが言う。「おかしなことだわね」
　そのとき急に、ロジャーズが部屋に入ってきた。
　「おそれいりますが、どなたか浴室のカーテンをご存じないでしょうか？」と訊く。「なくなったんです！　一階の浴室に赤いカーテンがかかっていたのですが——消えてしまったのです！」
　「今朝はあったのかね？」判事が尋ねた。
　「はい、ございました」
　「どうってことないだろう」とブロア。「赤いカーテンで人は殺せないよ」

　「はい、さようでございますね」ロジャーズは背を向けて去ったが、ぶるぶると震えていた。客たちはまたお茶を飲みだしたものの、不安そうに視線を交わしあった。

Chapter Ten

The next day, Lombard woke up late, at around ten o'clock in the morning.

"Funny I haven't been called to breakfast," he thought. He got dressed, went out, and knocked on Blore's door. When Blore answered, it was clear he had been asleep.

"It's almost 10:30," said Lombard.

"Is it? I didn't think I'd sleep so late," said Blore.

"Rogers hasn't been by to bring tea or breakfast, eh?"

"No," said Blore.

Lombard knocked on the others' doors. Armstrong was already up, and Emily Brent's room was empty. He had to wake both the judge and Vera. But no one had seen Rogers that morning.

Lombard went to Rogers's room and saw that the bed had been slept in. It was clear he had gotten up that morning, but where was he?

■wake up late 寝坊する、寝過ごす　■empty 形〔室内・道路などが〕誰もいない
■sleep in ～で寝る

第10章

　翌日、ロンバードは寝すごして午前10時頃に目を覚ました。

　「おかしいな。朝食に呼ばれなかったぞ」と思った。彼は着替えて部屋を
出、ブロアの部屋をノックした。ブロアの返事を聞くと、明らかに眠って
いたらしい。

　「もう10時30分だぜ」ロンバートは言った。

　「もう？　そんなに遅くまで寝てたとはね」とブロアが言う。

　「ロジャーズがお茶か朝食を持ってこなかったかい？」

　「いや、来てないな」とブロア。

　ロンバードは他の客たちの部屋をノックした。アームストロングはもう
起きており、エミリー・ブレントの部屋は誰もいない。判事とヴェラは起
こさなければならなかった。しかし、今朝は誰もロジャーズを見ていない
という。

　ロンバードはロジャーズの部屋を見にいった。すると、ベッドに横になっ
た跡があった。今朝、彼がここで起きたのはたしかだ。だが、いったいど
こにいるのだろう？

Lombard went downstairs, gathering Vera, Blore, Armstrong, and the judge as he went. As they entered the hall, Miss Brent came in from the front door.

"It's still raining and the sea is high," she said. "I doubt any boat will come for us today."

"Were you wandering around outside by yourself?" asked Blore. "Don't you know that's dangerous?"

"Mr. Blore," said Miss Brent, "I was keeping a sharp watch, I assure you."

"Have you seen Rogers?" he asked.

Miss Brent looked surprised.

"No, I haven't. Why?"

Then there was a scream from the dining room. Everyone rushed to the open door to see Vera pointing at the table.

"The soldiers!" she cried.

There were only six soldiers in the middle of the table.

* * *

They found Rogers shortly afterwards. He was by the garden shed. He had been cutting sticks with an ax to light the kitchen fire. A larger ax was leaning against the shed, one side of it covered with blood. Rogers lay on the ground, a deep wound in the back of his head.

■doubt 動～ではなさそうだと思う ■wander 動歩き回る、ぶらつく ■keep a sharp watch しっかり警戒する、十分気をつける ■I assure you. 確かです。断言できます。 ■shed 名物置小屋、納屋 ■ax 名おの ■wound 名外傷、創傷

ロンバードは、ヴェラ、ブロア、アームストロング、そして判事を呼び集めながら、一階へ下りた。ホールに入ると、ミス・ブレントが玄関から入ってきた。

　「まだ雨が降っているし、波も高いですね」彼女は言った。「今日もボートは来てくれないでしょう」

　「ひとりで外を歩きまわってたんですか？」ブロアが訊いた。「どれほど危険か、わかってるんですか」

　「ブロアさん」とミス・ブレント。「わたしは十分気をつけています。大丈夫ですよ」

　「ロジャーズを見ましたか？」ブレアが訊いた。

　ミス・ブレントは驚いた顔をした。

　「いいえ。どうしてそんなことを？」

　そのとき、ダイニングルームから悲鳴があがった。みんなが駆けよってドアをあけると、ヴェラがテーブルを指していた。

　「兵隊が！」ヴェラが叫ぶ。

　テーブルの真ん中には、6つの兵隊しかなかった。

＊　＊　＊

　ほどなくして、ロジャーズが見つかった。彼は物置小屋のそばにいた。台所の火を起こすために薪を割っていたらしい。そして、大きいほうの斧が小屋に立てかけられており、その刃の片面が血まみれになっていた。ロジャーズは地面に倒れ、後頭部に深い傷があった。

As the group stared in shock, Vera suddenly started to laugh.

"Do they keep bees on the island?" she asked between fits of laughter.

Everybody else looked at each other. It was as if the girl was going crazy right before their very eyes.

"Don't look at me like that!" Vera shouted. "I'm not crazy. It's that rhyme that's hanging up in our rooms! It's there for us to look at every day!"

Vera started laughing again, then said the lines from memory: *"Seven little soldier boys cutting up sticks. Six little soldier boys playing with a hive.* Well? Are there bee hives on this island?" She started laughing again.

Dr. Armstrong went to the girl, raised his hand, and hit her across the cheek. Vera gasped, shook her head, and stood silent for a moment.

"Thank you…I'm all right now," she said. She turned to Miss Brent. "Would you like to help me get breakfast ready?"

* * *

As the two women headed to the kitchen, Blore turned to Lombard.

"That young lady—she's losing her mind," Blore said.

■fit of ～の発作　■right before one's very eyes（人）のすぐ目の前で　■hit someone across ~ （人）の～を殴る、ぶつ

みなはショックを受けて、その光景を見つめた。すると、ヴェラが突然笑いだした。

「島ではハチを飼ってるの？」と、笑いの発作の合間に訊く。

他の者たちは顔を見合わせた。自分たちの目の前で、ヴェラが狂っていく。

「そんな目で見ないで！」ヴェラは叫んだ。「狂ってなんかいないわ。ほら、部屋にかかってるあの詩よ！　毎日見てるじゃないの！」

ヴェラはまた笑いだし、詩を思い出しながら言った。「『7人の小さな兵隊さんが薪を割っていたよ。6人の小さな兵隊さんがハチの巣で遊んでいたよ』ほらね？　この島にハチの巣はあるの？」そしてまた、げらげらと笑いだした。

アームストロング医師がつかつかと近づき、片手を振りあげてヴェラの頬をぶった。すると、彼女ははっと息をのんで、頭を振り、しばらくぼんやりと立っていた。

「ありがとうございます……もう大丈夫です」ヴェラはそう言うと、ミス・ブレントのほうに向きなおった。「朝食の用意を手伝っていただけますか？」

＊　＊　＊

ふたりの女が台所のほうへ去っていくと、ブロアがロンバードに顔を向けた。

「あのお嬢さんは——正気を失っているようだね」とブロアは言った。

"We're under a lot of stress here. People are being murdered all around us! Of course it's affecting her mental state," replied Lombard.

"But what if it was her mental state *before* she came to the island? We're looking for a crazy person, aren't we?"

"Yes…" said Lombard.

"Or the other woman! So neat and stiff! She never shows her feelings, does she? I know elderly women like that go crazy all the time! Especially a religious one like her. She probably thinks she's a messenger of God or something, and came to this island to punish us all!"

"Then again, *you* might be the killer," said Lombard. "You did lie in court and put that man in jail, didn't you? You sent him to his death."

"Yes, I admit it," said Blore. "Landor was innocent. But you see his gang threatened me. I had to lay the blame on Landor. Plus, they paid me…"

"None of us here are angels," said Lombard. "And I just noticed something we share in common. We're all guilty of crimes, but the law can't actually prove them. How interesting…"

* * *

After breakfast, Judge Wargrave spoke to the group.

■neat 形 きちんとした、整った　■stiff 形 堅苦しい　■religious 形 信心深い、敬虔な
■threaten 動 脅迫する　■lay the blame on 罪を（人）に着せる　■in common 共通
の、共通して

「みんな、ひどいストレスを受けているんだ。いたるところで人が殺されてるんだからな！　精神が不安定になるのも当然さ」ロンバードが答えた。

「でも、彼女の精神状態が、島に来るまえからおかしいのだったら？　わたしたちは狂人を探してるんじゃないのか？」

「ああ、そうだな……」とロンバード。

「それか、もうひとりの女だ！　彼女は潔癖症で頑固者だ！　感情さえ見せないじゃないか。ああいう年寄り女は、たいてい頭がおかしくなるんだよ。とくに彼女のような信心深い女はね。たぶん自分のことを神の使いか何かだと思いこんで、わたしたちを罰するためにこの島へやってきたんだよ！」

「だけどね、あんただって人殺しかもしれないんだぜ」ロンバードが言った。「あんたは法廷でうその証言をして、その男を刑務所に送ったんだろ？　あんたが死に追いやったわけだ」

「まあ、認めるよ」ブロアは言った。「ランドーは無実だった。しかしね、ギャングの一味に脅されたんだよ。彼に罪を着せるしかなかった。それに、金を出すとも……」

「ここにいるやつは、ひとりも天使じゃないってことか」とロンバード。「これで、みんなの共通点がわかったよ。全員有罪なのに、法律では実際に立証できないんだ。へえ、おもしろいじゃないか……」

＊　＊　＊

朝食が終わると、ウォーグレイヴ判事がみんなに話しかけた。

"We should talk about this morning's events," he said. "Let's all meet in the drawing room in thirty minutes."

Everybody agreed, and Vera started to clear away the plates. Emily Brent rose to help but had to sit back down.

"Oh!" she said. "I'm feeling rather dizzy."

The others either went to the kitchen to help clean or wandered out. Soon, Miss Brent was the only one left in the dining room.

Suddenly, she began to feel very sleepy. It occurred to her that there was a strange noise coming from the window. She turned her sleepy eyes to the window and listened harder. It was a buzzing, like a bee.

There was somebody in the room…but she couldn't turn around, couldn't call out. She was so sleepy…Then she felt the pain—the bee sting on the side of her neck…

* * *

Thirty minutes later, others had gathered in the drawing room and were waiting for Miss Brent.

"Shall I go get her?" asked Vera.

"If she's still not feeling well, we should go to her in the dining room," said Wargrave.

■sit back down 腰を下ろす、座り込む　■listen hard 耳を澄ます、よく聞く
■buzzing 图 ブーンという音　■call out 叫ぶ、呼びかける

「今朝の事件について、話し合うべきじゃないかね」と言う。「30分後に客間に集まるとしよう」

　誰もが賛成し、ヴェラが皿を片づけだした。エミリー・ブレントも手伝おうと立ちあがったが、思わずすわりこんだ。

　「ああ！　なんだか目まいがするわ」

　他の者たちは皿洗いを手伝いに台所へ行ったり、ぶらりと出ていったりした。やがて、ミス・ブレントはダイニングルームにひとりきりになった。

　そのとたん、彼女はひどい眠気に襲われた。窓から妙な音が聞こえるような気がする。眠い目を窓に向けて、耳をすました。ブーンとうなる羽音。ハチのようだ。

　誰かが部屋の中にいる……でも振りむくことも、声をあげることもできない。ああ、とても眠い……。そのとき、ちくりと痛みを感じた——首の横をハチに刺されたわ……。

＊　＊　＊

　30分後、他の者たちが客間に集まり、ミス・ブレントを待っていた。

　「呼んできましょうか？」ヴェラが訊いた。

　「彼女の具合が悪いのなら、われわれがダイニングルームへ行ったほうがいいだろう」ウォーグレイヴ判事が言った。

They found Miss Brent still sitting in her chair. From the back, nothing looked wrong. But then they saw her face—her blue lips and staring eyes.

"She's dead!" cried Blore.

Armstrong rushed to her.

"There's a mark here, on the side of her neck," he announced. "It's the mark of a syringe."

There was a buzzing sound from the window.

"Look!" Vera cried out, pointing. "It's a bee! Remember what I said this morning!"

"Well, it wasn't a bee sting that killed her. Somebody poisoned her with the syringe," said Armstrong. "It was probably cyanide, just like with Tony Marston."

"Did anybody bring a syringe to this island?" the judge asked.

After an uncomfortable silence, Dr. Armstrong said, "I did."

There was an uproar, and the group demanded to see it. Dr. Armstrong led the others to his room and emptied his bag onto his bed. The syringe was not there.

*   *   *

"Somebody must have taken it!" cried Armstrong.

There was silence in the room. Finally, Wargrave spoke.

■look wrong おかしい[間違っている]ように見える　■syringe 图《医》(皮下) 注射器
■uproar 图騒動、大騒ぎ、わめき叫ぶ声　■empty 動〔容器などから中身を〕出す

ダイニングルームへ行くと、ミス・ブレントはまだ椅子にすわっていた。後ろからだと、なんともないように見える。ところが顔を見ると——唇が紫色になり、目が大きく見開いていた。

　「死んでいる！」ブロアが叫んだ。

　アームストロングが駆けよった。

　「ここに跡がある、首の横だ」彼は告げた。「注射の跡だな」

　窓の外から羽音が聞こえた。

　「見て！」ヴェラが指さして叫んだ。「ハチよ！　わたしが今朝言ったとおりでしょ！」

　「いや、ハチに刺されて亡くなったのではないよ。誰かが注射器で毒を注入したんだ」とアームストロング。「おそらく青酸カリだろう。トニー・マーストン君のときと同じだ」

　「誰かこの島に注射器を持ってきたかね？」判事が訊いた。

　アームストロング医師は気まずそうに黙りこんでから、「持ってきましたよ」と言った。

　みんなが騒ぎだし、口々に注射器を見せろと迫った。そこでアームストロング医師は彼らを自分の部屋へ連れていき、かばんの中身をベッドの上に空けてみせた。ところが、注射器はなかったのだ。

＊　＊　＊

　「きっと盗まれたんだ！」アームストロングは叫んだ。

　部屋の中が、しんとなった。ようやくウォーグレイヴが口を開いた。

"There are five of us here. *One of us is a murderer.* We must do everything we can to protect the four who are innocent. Dr. Armstrong, what medicine did you bring here?"

"You can search my medicine bag," said Armstrong. "I only brought some sleeping medicine, aspirin—nothing harmful!"

"I also have some sleeping medicine," said the judge. "I say anything that could be harmful—the gun, these medicines—should be locked away. Let's search everybody here and take away anything that might be harmful."

Everybody agreed and they went into Lombard's room next. Lombard went to his table where he kept his gun and opened the drawer. His eyes grew wide.

"The gun...It's not here."

"Liar!" shouted Blore.

"I swear, this is where I keep it! Somebody stole it!" Lombard shouted back.

"Calm down," cut in Wargrave. "We'll search for it. Right now, let's collect everything else that might be harmful."

They went into each person's room and searched from top to bottom, but they did not find the gun or anything else that could possibly cause harm.

■aspirin 名アスピリン《鎮痛・解熱剤》 ■harmful 形有害な、危険を及ぼす ■lock away しまい込む、鍵をかけて保管する ■eyes grow wide 目を見開く、目を皿(のよう)にする ■Liar! うそつき！ ■from top to bottom〔場所・空間などの〕一番上から下まで、あらゆるところに

「ここには5人しかいない。その中のひとりが殺人者なのだ。無実の4人を守るために、できるかぎりのことをしなければならん。アームストロング先生、ここにはどんな薬を持ってきたのですかな？」

　「わたしの薬剤バッグを調べてみてください」とアームストロング。「睡眠薬とアスピリンだけです——危険なものなどありませんよ！」

　「睡眠薬ならわたしも持っている」と判事。「そこで提案だが、危険になり得るものは——ピストルや、これらの薬なども——鍵をかけてしまっておいてはどうかね。全員を調べて、危険になり得るものを取りあげることにしよう」

　全員が賛成し、今度はロンバードの部屋へ行った。ロンバードはピストルをしまってあるテーブルに近づいて、引き出しをあけた。そのとたん、目を大きく見開いた。

　「ピストルが……ないぞ」

　「うそつきめ！」ブロアが怒鳴った。

　「本当にここにしまってたさ！　誰かに盗まれたんだ！」ロンバードは怒鳴りかえした。

　「落ち着くんだ」ウォーグレイヴが割りこんだ。「あとで探すとしよう。とにかくいまは、他に危険になりそうなものをすべて集めるんだ」

　彼らはそれぞれの部屋に入って隅から隅まで探したが、ピストルや、他に危害を与えそうなものは見つからなかった。

Gathering up the medicine, they went down to the kitchen, where there was a large silver box with a lock and key. They put everything in the box and locked it.

"Who will keep the key?" asked Blore.

"This closet has a lock," said Wargrave. He put the locked box into the closet and locked the door. Then he gave the box key to Lombard and the closet key to Blore.

"You two are the strongest here," he said. "It will be very difficult for either of you to take the key from the other, and it would be impossible for the rest of us."

"I've been thinking," said Dr. Armstrong, "and I don't know where the gun could be, but I think I know where the syringe is." He led the way outside and around the house. Near the dining room window, he found the syringe and the sixth soldier figure.

"Of course," said Blore. "After killing Miss Brent, the killer threw the needle and the figure out the window."

"We should look for the gun again," said Vera.

They searched the entire house without result. The gun was still missing.

■gather up 集める ■throw ~ out the window ～を窓から放り投げる ■without result 成果もなく ■missing 形〔あるはずの物が〕見つからない

薬を集めて台所へ下りていくと、錠と鍵のついた大きな銀製の箱があった。その箱に薬をぜんぶ入れ、鍵をかけた。

「誰が鍵を持っておくんです？」ブロアが尋ねた。

「このクローゼットには鍵がかかるのだよ」ウォーグレイヴはそう言うと、箱をクローゼットに入れて、扉に鍵をかけた。それから、箱の鍵をロンバードに、クローゼットの鍵をブロアに渡した。

「きみたちふたりは、この中でいちばん強いからね」と言う。「どちらかが相手から鍵を奪うのは難しいはずだ。もちろん、われわれ残りの者には無理だろう」

「ちょっと考えてたんですけどね」アームストロング医師が言った。「ピストルがどこにあるかはさっぱりわからないが、注射器のある場所なら見当がつきますよ」彼は外へ出て、家の周囲をまわった。するとダイニングルームの窓の近くで、注射器と、6個目の兵隊の人形が見つかった。

「なるほど」とブロア。「ミス・ブレントを殺したあと、犯人は注射器と人形を窓から投げ捨てたんだな」

「もう一度ピストルを探したほうがいいわ」ヴェラが言った。

　彼らは家中をくまなく調べたが、無駄だった。ピストルは見つからないままだ。

覚えておきたい英語表現

> Dr. Armstrong ran to Marston, **who** lay on the ground.
> (p. 82, 1行目)
>
> アームストロング医師が、床に倒れたマーストンに駆けよった。

【解説】Marston についての「補足説明」をするとき、関係代名詞の前にカンマ(,)を置いて、表記します。これを英文法で、「関係代名詞の非制限用法」と言います。

ふつう皆さんは、カンマ(,)やピリオド(.)について、ほとんど無関心だと思いますが、関係代名詞のときだけは、少し意識してほしいと思います。関係代名詞の「非制限用法」というものがあります。簡単に言ってしまえば、ある「人物」や「名詞」に追加の説明を加えるときに用います。

具体例を本文から抜き出してみましょう。

> "We'll take you to the boat, **which** will take you to the island."
> (p. 32, 5行目)
> (わたしたちがみなさんをボートまでお送りします。それからボートが島までお連れすることになります)

まず、ボートについて言います。そして、「そのボートは」と補足情報をつけ加えるときに、〈カンマ + 関係代名詞〉を使います。

もう一つ、例を見てみましょう。Vera について、補足説明を加えています。

> "Not yet," said Vera, **who** had been outside with Lombard and Blore.
> (p. 92, 8行目)
> (「いいえ、まだです」ヴェラが言った。彼女はロンバードとブロアといっしょに外に出ていたのだ)

それでは、カンマがあるか、ないかでどんな違いがあるのか見ていきましょう。

(1) I have two sisters **who** live in Kyoto.
   (私は、京都に住んでいる姉が二人います)

（2）　I have two sisters**, who** live in Kyoto.
（私は、二人の姉がいて、二人とも京都に住んでいます）

　（1）の英文からだけだと、他に「大阪に住んでいる姉」がいるかもしれません。つまり、二人の姉以外にも姉妹、兄弟がいる可能性があります。

　（2）の英文は、まず「二人の姉がいます」と言って、追加説明として、「二人は京都に住んでいます」という意味を表します。

　カンマ（,）は小さいですが、関係代名詞のときだけは、大きな差を生み出していまします。

　追加情報を一つ。上の（1）（2）の例文でわかるように、人の名前や地名といった「固有名詞」のあとの関係代名詞は、この世で一つしかないので、必ず、カンマをつけます。非制限用法を使うわけです。

This is the Akita dog Masaru**, which** lives in Russia.
（これは秋田犬のマサルです。そして、ロシアに住んでいます）

Last year I visited Shuri Castle**, which** was burned down in 2019.
（去年、首里城を訪れましたが、2019年に焼失してしまいました）

　一つ大切なことを言い忘れていました。この非制限用法は、同じ関係代名詞でもthatのときは使えないのです。つまり〈カンマ＋that〉はありません。関係代名詞の前にカンマが使えるのは、以下の4つです。

　　〈カンマ＋who〉
　　〈カンマ＋which〉
　　〈カンマ＋whose〉
　　〈カンマ＋whom〉

　あとは、関係副詞のwhenとwhereの2つで、合計6つです。少ないので覚えてしまいましょう。

> "Liar!" shouted Blore. <small>（p. 140, 下から8行目）</small>
> 「うそつきめ！」ブロアが怒鳴った。

【解説】日本人が軽い気持ちで使いがちな表現に、「ウソ！」とか「うそつき」という言葉があります。英語で言うと、lieとか、liarというわけですが、これらは、英米では人間関係を壊してしまうほどの強烈な意味を持った言葉ですので、不用意に使うことがないように注意しておきましょう。

「ウソをつく」は英語でtell a lieと言います。「一つのウソ」ですが、一つウソをつくと、もっとたくさんのウソを重ねることになるかもしれません。複数形を使って、tell liesという表現もあります。

さて、逆の意味の「真実を言う」は、なんと言うでしょうか？　答えは、tell the truthです。真実は1つしかないのですが、tell a truthとは言わず、「（誰もが知っている、あの）本当のこと」という意味を表すtheを使って、tell the truthとなるのです。

英語を使ったことで、人間関係を壊してしまったら元も子もありません。「ウソー！」と言いたいときは、「本当なの？」という意味のReally? を使うと無難です。

　　　Rob:　　I love you, Kyoko.　（京子、大好きだよ）
　　　Kyoko: Really? Thank you.　（ウソー！ ありがとう）

And Then
There Were None

Part 3

Chapter Eleven

Five people sat in the drawing room, watching each other, suspecting each other, yet needing each other for protection. They had decided that they would do everything as a group. Only one person could leave the group at a time. The other four would remain together until the fifth person returned.

It was pouring rain again.

"Once the weather clears, we can make a bonfire, or signal to the village, or do something to get a boat to come to us," said Lombard.

They had eaten lunch together—more food out of cans in the kitchen closet—but it was a silent meal. Each person's mind raced with terrible thoughts.

"It's Armstrong...I saw him looking at me just now...He's probably not a doctor at all, but a madman escaped from some mental hospital!"

■at a time 一度に、同時に ■remain 動〔ある場所に〕残る、とどまる ■pouring rain 土砂降りの雨 ■bonfire 图 たき火

第11章

　5人は客間にすわり、たがいに疑いの目で見つめあっていた。それでも身を守るためには、おたがいが必要だ。そこで、何をするにも団体行動をとることにした。みんなから離れられるのは、いっときにひとりずつ。他の4人は、5人目が戻るまでいっしょに待つのである。

　ふたたび雨が強くなってきた。
　「天気がよくなったら、たき火をたくなり、村に合図するなりして、なんとかボートを呼べるさ」ロンバードが言った。

　昼食は、台所のクローゼットから缶詰の食料を出して、みんなでいっしょにすませたが、むっつりと黙ったままの食事だった。それぞれの頭の中では、おそろしい考えが駆けめぐっていた。
　（きっとアームストロングよ……ついさっきも、わたしを見ていたもの……もしかしたら、お医者さまなんかじゃなくて、精神病院から逃げてきた狂人かもしれないわ！）

"They won't get me; I know how to take care of myself! But where the devil is my gun? *Somebody knows where it is...*"

"Everyone is going crazy...They're all afraid of death. *I'm* afraid of death. But that won't stop death from coming...The girl. Yes, I'll watch the girl..."

"It's only twenty to four! Has time stopped moving? Oh, God, I'm going crazy. Something is happening to my head..."

"I must stay calm...I must stay calm. I've got everything planned out. But which one? I think...Yes, I think *him*."

When the clock struck five they all jumped. They realized that the room had grown dark around them. Lombard got up to turn on the lights, but they did not come on.

"Of course!" he said. "The engine hasn't run today since Rogers never saw to it. I suppose we can go out and get it going."

"I saw some candles in the kitchen," said Wargrave. "We better just use those."

"I'll go get them," said Lombard. He went into the kitchen and came back with a box of candles. They lit them, put them around the room, and continued to sit.

■devil 图〈強意語〉一体（全体）　■stay calm 平静を保つ　■plan out 計画を練る
■strike 動〔時計が正時などを〕音で知らせる

（おれはやられないぞ。身を守るすべを知ってるんだからな！ だけど、おれのピストルはいったいどこにあるんだ？ 誰かが知ってるはずだぞ……）

（みんな狂ってしまうだろう……死ぬのが怖いからだ。わたしも死ぬのは怖い。でも、死が近づくのを止めることはできないのだ……。あの娘か。そうだ、あの娘を見張ろう……）

（まだ4時20分前か！ 時間が止まったのか？ ああ、まったく、気が変になりそうだ。頭の中で何かが起こっている……）

（落ち着かねば……落ち着かねばならん。すべて計画ずみだ。しかし、誰が？ そうだな……そう、彼だ）

時計が5時を打ったとき、みんなは飛びあがった。いつのまにか部屋が暗くなっている。ロンバードが立ちあがって電灯のスイッチを入れたが、つかなかった。

「ああ、そうか！」彼は言った。「今日は発電機が動いてないんだ。ロジャーズがつけてないからな。みんなで外へ出て、発電機を動かそう」

「たしか、台所にろうそくがあったはずだ」ウォーグレイヴが言った。「あれを使うほうがいいだろう」

「じゃあ、おれが取ってくる」ロンバードは台所へ行き、ろうそくの箱を持って戻ってきた。ろうそくを灯して部屋中に置くと、彼らはまたすわりつづけた。

At around six o'clock, Vera felt she could not sit any longer. She took a candle and said she was going to her room to wash her face with cold water. She left the four men in the drawing room and went upstairs. When she opened the door to her room, a curious smell met her nose. It was the smell of the sea!

"Can I swim out to the island, Miss Claythorne? Why can't I swim out to the island?"

Awful, whining little brat!

Hugo was watching her . . .

She took a step forward, smelling the sea, when a cold, wet hand touched her face. Vera screamed and screamed.

✳ ✳ ✳

Vera did not hear the men rush up to her room. She did not hear them yelling her name as they came up the steps. Only when she saw candles in the doorway did she come to her senses.

"Are you all right?" the men asked.

"Good God, look at that!"

Hanging from the ceiling from a black hook was a long, wide ribbon of seaweed.

■curious 形 気になる、奇妙な　■brat 名〈侮蔑的〉（うるさい・行儀の悪い）子ども、ちび　■take a step forward 一歩前に進む、一歩踏み出す　■doorway 名 戸口　■come to one's senses 正気に戻る、意識を回復する　■Good God! なんてことだ！　■seaweed 名 海草、海藻

6時頃になると、ヴェラはもうすわっていられなくなった。ろうそくを1
本手に取り、自分の部屋へ行って冷たい水で顔を洗いたいと言った。そして
4人の男たちを客間に残し、2階へ上がっていった。自分の部屋のドアをあ
けると、鼻をつく奇妙なにおいがした。ああ、これは、海のにおいだわ！

　「島まで泳いでいい、クレイソーン先生？　どうして島まで泳いじゃだめ
なの？」

　うっとうしい、めそめそしてばかりのおちびさん！

　ヒューゴーがわたしをじっと見つめている……。

　ヴェラは海のにおいをかぎながら、一歩前に踏みだした。すると、冷た
く濡れた手が彼女の顔にふれた。ヴェラは悲鳴をあげた。ひたすら叫びつ
づけた。

＊　＊　＊

　男たちが彼女の部屋へと走りだしたが、ヴェラには聞こえなかった。階
段を駆け上がりながら名前を呼ぶ声も、耳に入らない。戸口にろうそくの
火が見えたとき、ようやくヴェラは正気を取りもどした。

　「大丈夫ですか？」男たちが訊いた。

　「ああ、あんまりよ、あれを見て！」

　天井の黒いフックからぶらさがっているのは、長くて幅の広い帯状の海
草だった。

It was only seaweed that had touched her face! She had thought it was the cold, dead hand of Cyril Hamilton! Vera broke into wild, crazy laughter.

"Only seaweed! Only seaweed!" she said, over and over.

"She needs a drink," Lombard said. "I'll get a bottle of brandy."

When Lombard returned with the brandy, Vera took a drink and began to feel a little better. Suddenly, she noticed there were only three men in the room.

"Where's the judge?" she asked.

The men looked at each other.

"That's odd...I thought he came up with us."

"I thought he was right behind me," said Armstrong. "Of course he'd be slower than us. He's an old man."

As they went down the stairs, Armstrong called out, "Wargrave, where are you?"

There was no answer. There was only the sound of the storm.

■over and over 何度もくり返して ■right behind ～のすぐ後ろに ■no answer 返事がない

顔にふれたのは、ただの海草だったのね！　シリル・ハミルトンの冷たい死人の手だと思ったのに！　ヴェラは狂ったように、けたたましく笑った。

「ただの海草！　ただの海草よ！」何度も何度もそう言う。
「何か飲ませるしかないな」とロンバード。「ブランデーを取ってこよう」

　ロンバードがブランデーを持って戻ってきたので、ヴェラは一口飲んだ。少し気分が落ち着いてくる。すると、部屋に男が3人しかいないことに気がついた。
「判事さんはどこなの？」ヴェラは訊いた。
　男たちは顔を見合わせた。
「おかしいな……いっしょに上がってきたと思ったのに」
「わたしのすぐ後ろにいたと思うが」とアームストロング。「もちろん、わたしたちより足が遅いだろう。なにしろ年だからね」
　みんなで階段を下り、アームストロングが呼びかけた。「ウォーグレイヴさん、どこですか？」
　返事がない。聞こえるのは、嵐の音だけだ。

When they got to the drawing room, they saw him sitting in his chair. He had on what looked like a gray wig and a red robe. Armstrong held the others back, and he went toward the old man.

He lifted the wig off the judge's head. Under it, in the middle of the forehead, was a round, red mark.

"He's been shot!" said Armstrong.

"My God! The gun!" cried Blore.

Vera went over and picked up the wig from the floor.

"Miss Brent's gray yarn..." she said.

"And the red bathroom curtain!" cried Blore. "This is what they were for!"

Suddenly Philip Lombard broke into wild laughter and cried out, *"Five little soldier boys going in for law; one got in Chancery and then there were Four!"*

■wig 图〔はげを隠すまたは儀式のための〕かつら　■hold someone back（人）の行動を制する、（人）を前に進めなくする　■forehead 图額、前面

客間まで来ると、ウォーグレイヴが椅子にすわっているのが見えた。灰色のかつらと赤いローブのようなものを身につけている。アームストロングは他の者たちを手で制して、判事に近づいていった。

　判事の頭からかつらを持ちあげる。そのすぐ下の額の真ん中に、丸くて赤い跡があった。
　「撃たれている！」アームストロングは言った。
　「なんてことだ！　あのピストルだな！」ブロアが叫んだ。
　ヴェラが入っていき、床からかつらを拾いあげた。
　「ブレントさんの灰色の毛糸よ……」
　「それに浴室の赤いカーテンだ！」ブロアが声をあげる。「このために盗ったんだな！」
　すると突然、フィリップ・ロンバードが声高に笑いだし、大声で言った。「『5人の小さな兵隊さんが法律を学んでいたよ。ひとりが大法院に入って4人になった』というわけさ！」

Chapter Twelve

They carried Judge Wargrave to his bed and gathered in the hall. They didn't know what to do.

"Only four of us now..." said Blore. "Who'll be the next?"

"How did it happen?" said Armstrong.

"It was very clever!" burst out Lombard. "That seaweed was put in Miss Claythorne's room as a distraction! Everyone runs up there thinking *she's* been murdered, and in the confusion, someone gets to the old man!"

"Why didn't anyone hear the shot?"

"Miss Claythorne was screaming, it's storming, we were running around and yelling," said Lombard.

They all fell silent and eyed each other again with new suspicions.

"I'm going to bed," said Vera.

■not know what to do 何をしたらよいのかわからない ■clever 形利口な、賢い、巧みな ■distraction 图注意をそらすもの、気を散らすこと ■confusion 图混乱状態 ■get to ～に取りかかる、～に到達する

第12章

　みんなはウォーグレイヴ判事をベッドに運んでから、ホールに集まった。どうしたらいいのか、もうわからなかった。

　「これで4人だけになった……」ブロアが言った。「次は誰だろう？」

　「どうしてこんなことになったんだ？」とアームストロング。

　「まったく、うまいやり方だぜ！」ロンバードが急に大声を出した。「クレイソーンさんの部屋に海草をぶらさげたのは、おれたちの気をそらすためだったんだ！　みんな、彼女が殺されたと思って、2階へ走っていった。そして大騒ぎしているあいだに、誰かがあのじいさんを殺したのさ！」

　「どうして誰も銃声に気づかなかったんだろう？」

　「クレイソーンさんが悲鳴をあげていたし、外は嵐だ。おれたちも走りまわったり、怒鳴ったりしてたじゃないか」とロンバード。

　彼らは黙りこみ、新たな疑惑を抱いて、おたがいを見つめあった。

　「わたし、もう寝るわ」ヴェラが言った。

"Me too," said Lombard.

All four people went upstairs to their room, and all four people shut and locked their door. All four people had trouble going to sleep.

*　*　*

Lombard took off his clothes, getting ready for bed. He felt uneasy without his gun. He went to the table and opened the drawer again. His mouth dropped open when he saw his gun there. Somebody had taken it...then returned it!

*　*　*

Blore was lying in bed awake when he thought he heard something outside his door. He got up and went quietly to the door to listen. He listened hard for a long time, but he did not hear anything again.

"Am I just imagining things?" he thought. Then he heard it again. Footsteps came from further down the hall, where the others' rooms were. They passed Blore's door and went down the stairs. Suddenly, Blore realized why he could hear things so well: the storm was over.

■have trouble〔~するのに〕苦労する　■uneasy 形 不安な、心配な　■drop open 意図しないで開ける　■imagining things《be ~》思い過ごしだ、気のせいだ　■further 形 さらに遠い[隔たった]　■be over 終わって、おしまいになって

「おれもだ」とロンバード。

　4人は2階へ上がって寝室に入り、みなドアを閉めて鍵をかけた。そして4人とも、まんじりともせず夜をすごした。

＊　＊　＊

　ロンバードは服を脱いで寝ようとした。でも、ピストルがなくて不安だった。テーブルへ近寄り、もう一度引き出しをあけてみる。驚いて口をぽかんとあけた。ピストルがあるではないか。誰かが盗んで……それから戻したのだ！

＊　＊　＊

　ブロアは眠れないまま、ベッドに横になっていた。すると、ドアの外で何か聞こえたような気がした。ぱっと起きあがり、静かにドアに近づいて耳をそばだてる。かなりのあいだ耳をすましてみた。だが、もう何も聞こえてこない。

　「ただの思い過ごしかな？」そう思ったとき、ふたたび音がした。足音が近づいてくる。廊下の向こう、他の者の部屋があるほうからだ。足音はブロアの部屋の前を通りすぎて、階段を下りていく。ふいに、こんなにはっきりと音が聞こえる理由がわかった。嵐がやんだのだ。

Blore grabbed a heavy lamp, opened his door, and stepped out into the hall without a sound. He went down the stairs and saw a figure going out the front door. Then he had a thought: Was this a trap to lure him out of the house? But the killer had made a mistake, because now, of the three other rooms upstairs, *one must be empty!* All Blore had to do was go and see!

He went quickly back up the hall. He knocked quietly on Armstrong's door. There was no answer. Then he went to Lombard's room and knocked.

"Who's there?"

"It's Blore. I don't think Armstrong is in his room. Wait a minute."

He went to Vera's room and knocked.

"Yes?" came Vera's voice, full of fear.

"It's all right," said Blore. "I think Armstrong is the killer. Do *not* open your door unless both Lombard and I come to your door together, do you understand?"

■grab 動つかみ取る　■figure 名人影、姿　■lure 動〔人を〕おびき出す、誘惑する
■full of fear 不安でいっぱいである　■unless 接〜でない限り

ブロアは重いランプをつかむと、ドアをあけ、音も立てずに廊下に出た。階段を下りていくと、玄関から出ていく人影が見えた。そのとき、ふと思った。これは、わたしを外へおびきだそうとする罠<ruby>罠<rt>わな</rt></ruby>じゃないのか？　でも犯人はミスを犯したぞ。上にある他の3つの部屋のうち、ひとつは誰もいないはずだ！　見にいけばいいだけだ！

　ブロアはすばやく2階の廊下に戻った。そしてアームストロングの部屋をそっとノックした。返事がない。それからロンバードの部屋へ行き、ノックした。
　「誰だ？」
　「ブロアだよ。アームストロングが部屋にいないようだ。ちょっと待っててくれ」
　つぎにヴェラの部屋へ行き、ノックする。
　「どなた？」ヴェラのおびえた声がした。
　「大丈夫だよ」とブロア。「アームストロングが犯人のようなんだ。ロンバードとわたしがいっしょに来るまで、けっしてドアをあけないように。いいね？」

"Yes," came the answer.

Blore raced back to Lombard's room and explained the situation quickly.

Lombard's eyes lit up.

"So it's the doctor?" he said. Lombard went to Armstrong's door and knocked on it himself. Again, there was no answer.

"Ha! The game's up! Let's go catch him," he said. "And look what's been returned to me!" Lombard showed Blore the gun.

"You had it all along!" cried Blore, fresh fear in his eyes.

"I swear to you my gun was gone this afternoon and returned this evening. I don't know why he would return it, but it's to our advantage now," said Lombard. "I'll look for Armstrong alone if you won't come." With that, he ran down the stairs and out into the night. After a moment, Blore followed.

* * *

After what seemed like a long time, Vera heard steps in the house again. They went all over—downstairs, upstairs, even up into the attic. Then there were voices at her door. It was Lombard and Blore.

■race back 急いで引き返す　■all along〈話〉最初[初め]からずっと　■advantage 图好都合[有益]な点　■all over 至る所を、くまなく　■attic 图屋根裏(部屋)

「はい」と返事が聞こえる。

　ブロアは急いでロンバードの部屋へ戻り、手早く状況を説明した。

　ロンバードの目が光った。

　「じゃあ、犯人は先生なのか？」そう言うと、ロンバードはアームストロングの部屋へ行き、自分でノックしてみた。やはり、返事がない。

　「ハハ！　これでゲームは終わりだ！　やつを捕まえようぜ！」と言う。「ほら、これが返ってきたしな！」ロンバードはブロアにピストルを見せた。

　「きみは、それをずっと持ってたんだな！」ブロアが叫んだ。新たな恐怖が目に浮かぶ。

　「このピストルは今日の午後なくなって、夜に戻ってきたんだ。誓ってもいい。なんで返したのかわからんが、これがあれば、おれたちのほうが有利だ」とロンバード。「あんたが来ないなら、おれひとりでアームストロングを探しにいくぜ」そう言うと、ロンバードは階段を駆けおり、夜の中へ出ていった。しばらくして、ブロアも後を追った。

＊　＊　＊

　長い時間が過ぎたように感じる。ヴェラは、ふたたび家の中に足音がするのを耳にした。家中を歩きまわっている──1階、2階、そして屋根裏まで。それから、部屋の前で声がした。ロンバードとブロアだ。

"Vera! Are you there?"

"Yes. What happened?"

"Let us in."

Vera went to her door and carefully opened it. The two men stood outside, strange looks on their faces.

"Armstrong has disappeared!" said Lombard.

"What!" cried Vera.

"We looked everywhere," said Blore. "There's nowhere to hide on this island."

"He must have come back to the house!" Vera said.

"We looked," said Blore. "He's not here."

"It's true," said Lombard. "And there's one more thing: there are only three little soldier boys on the table."

■let someone in（人）を中に入れる［入れてやる］　■strange look (on one's face)
妙な［けげんな］表情

「ヴェラ！　いるかい？」

「ええ。何があったの？」

「中に入れてくれ」

　ヴェラはドアに近づき、用心しながらあけた。ふたりの男が、けげんそうな表情をして立っている。

「アームストロングが消えたんだ！」ロンバードが言った。

「なんですって！」ヴェラは声をあげた。

「あらゆるところを調べたが」とブロア。「この島にはもう隠れるところがない」

「じゃあ、きっと家に戻ってきたんだわ！」とヴェラ。

「それも見たが」とブロア。「ここにもいないんだよ」

「本当さ」ロンバードが言った。「それに、もうひとつ。テーブルの小さな兵隊が3つしかないんだ」

Chapter Thirteen

The next morning, three people ate a silent breakfast.

"The weather has cleared," said Lombard. "We can go outside and make light signals with a mirror. Maybe someone will see it and send a boat."

"The weather might be better but the water's still rough," said Blore. "They probably won't be able to send a boat until tomorrow. But more importantly, what happened to Armstrong?"

"Don't you see?" cut in Vera. *"Four little soldier boys going out to sea; A red herring swallowed one and then there were Three.* The 'red herring'! He took away the soldier figure to make you *think* he was killed. Armstrong is still on the island, and he's out to get us!"

"You might be right," said Lombard thoughtfully.

"That's rather giving himself away, isn't it?" said Blore. "He might have changed the rhyme so we wouldn't figure it out."

■rough 形〔天候などが〕荒れた　■take away 取り除く、持ち去る、取り上げる　■out to get 〜をやっつけようと躍起になって　■give oneself away 正体を現す、内心をさらけ出す

第13章

　翌朝、3人は黙々と朝食をとっていた。

　「やっと晴れたな」ロンバードが口を開いた。「外に出て、鏡を反射させて信号を送ろう。誰かが気づいて、ボートを寄こしてくれるかもしれない」

　「天気はよくなったが、まだ海が荒れているからね」とブロアが言った。「明日までボートを寄こすことはできないだろう。でも、もっと大事なことがあるよ。アームストロングは、いったいどうしたんだろう？」

　「わからないの？」ヴェラが口を挟んだ。「『4人の小さな兵隊さんが海に出ていたよ。1人が燻製のニシンにのまれて、3人になった』ほら、注意をそらすのに使う『燻製のニシン』*よ！　自分が殺されたと思わせるために、兵隊の人形を捨てたのよ。アームストロングはまだ島にいる。外にいて、わたしたちを殺そうとしているんだわ！」

　「きみの言うとおりかもしれないな」ロンバードが考えながら言った。

　「それじゃあ自分から正体をばらすようなものじゃないかな？」とブロア。「わからないように詩を変えておくのがふつうだろう」

---

*燻製のニシン:人の注意をそらすもの。猟犬を訓練するため、キツネの通り道に燻製のニシンを置き、キツネのにおいを消したことから生まれた慣用句。

"But he's crazy!" yelled Vera. "Tony Marston choking, Mrs. Rogers oversleeping, Rogers cutting sticks, that bee in the window—it's all crazy! It all has to fit with that childish rhyme!"

"What about the line about the zoo? '*A big bear hugged one and then there were Two.*' There's no zoo on the island," said Blore.

"*We're* the zoo!" cried Vera. "We're so mad with fear we're hardly human any more!"

* * *

They spent the morning on the cliff, taking turns holding the mirror up to the sun, making S.O.S. messages. Just after two o'clock, Blore said he had to eat something.

"Let's have some lunch," he said, "I feel weak. I need food."

"I'm not going back inside that house," said Vera. "I'm staying out here in the open, where I can see anyone coming near me."

Lombard agreed to stay with Vera, and Blore went alone to the house.

"Isn't it dangerous to go in there alone?" asked Vera.

"He made his own decision," said Lombard. "Besides, Blore is twice the size of Armstrong. I'm sure he can fight him off."

■fit with ～と一致する、ぴったり合う　■hardly 圓 ほとんど～ない、とても～ない 《notより弱い否定》　■take turn ~ing 交代で～する　■make one's own decision 自分の意志で決める　■twice the size of ～の2倍の大きさ　■fight off 撃退する

「でも、あの人は狂ってるのよ！」ヴェラは大声をあげる。「トニー・マーストンはのどをつまらせて、ミセス・ロジャーズは寝すごして、ロジャーズは薪を割ってて、そして窓にはハチがいて——何もかも気ちがいじみてるじゃない！ すべて、あの童謡のとおりじゃないといけないのよ！」

「だったら、動物園の行についてはどうだい？『1人が大きなクマに抱きしめられて、2人になった』というけど、島に動物園はないよ」とブロア。

「わたしたちが動物園なのよ！」ヴェラは叫んだ。「恐怖で頭がおかしくなって、もう人間とはいえないわ！」

＊　＊　＊

彼らは午前中崖の上に立ち、交替で鏡を太陽に向けて、SOSの信号を送った。2時過ぎになると、ブロアが何か食べたいと言いだした。

「昼食にしよう。なんだか力が出ない。腹がへったよ」

「わたしはもうあの家には戻らないわよ」ヴェラが言った。「この開けたところにいるわ。ここなら誰かが近づいてきても見えるから」

ロンバードもヴェラと残ると言ったので、ブロアはひとりで家に向かった。

「ひとりで中に入るのは危険じゃないかしら？」ヴェラが訊いた。

「ブロアが自分で決めたんだ」とロンバード。「それに、彼はアームストロングの倍ほど体が大きいからな。きっとやり返せるさ」

They sat quietly, looking at the ocean for sometime. Suddenly, they heard a distant cry.

"What was that?"

"It sounded like a cry for help," said Lombard. He felt his gun in his pocket and got up. The two went back to the house and walked all around it. On the east side, they found Blore. He was lying face-down on the ground, his head crushed by a great block of white marble. Lombard looked up.

"Whose window is that, just above?" he asked.

Trembling, and her voice a whisper, Vera said, "Mine. That was the marble clock on my shelf. It was shaped like a bear..."

"That settles it," said Lombard. "Armstrong is somewhere in that house. I'm going to get him."

"You can't go in there!" cried Vera. "That's exactly what he wants!"

"What can we do?"

"We must stay out here and wait. Somebody will come to get us."

"All right, but when night comes, we mustn't fall asleep," said Lombard. "Until then, let's walk to the top of the island to keep watch."

■for sometime しばらくの間　■distant 形遠い、遠く離れた　■lie face-down うつぶせに横たわる　■crush 動押しつぶす、ぺしゃんこにする　■just above ～の真上に[すぐ上に]　■mustn't〈省略形〉～してはいけない（＝ must not）

ふたりは静かにすわって、しばらく海を見つめていた。すると突然、遠くで叫び声がした。
　「あれは何？」
　「助けを求めてるようだったぞ」ロンバードはそう言うと、ポケットにピストルがあるのを確かめながら立ちあがった。ふたりは家へ戻り、まわりを歩いてみた。そして家の東側で、ブロアを発見した。うつぶせに倒れ、白い大理石の大きな塊で頭をつぶされている。ロンバードは上を見あげた。

　「すぐ上にあるのは、誰の部屋の窓だ？」と訊く。
　震えながら、ささやくようにヴェラが言った。「わたしのよ。あれは、棚にあった大理石の時計だわ。クマのような形をしていた……」
　「これで決まりだな」とロンバード。「アームストロングは家のどこかにいるんだ。おれが捕まえてやる」
　「入っちゃだめ！」ヴェラは声をあげた。「彼の思うつぼよ！」

　「じゃあ、どうするんだ？」
　「外で待つのよ。そのうち誰かが来てくれるわ」

　「わかったよ。だけど夜がきても、眠っちゃいけないぜ」とロンバード。「それまで、島のいちばん高いところまで行って見張ることにしよう」

They walked up to the very peak and stood, silently looking around. Their normal lives seemed so far away now, like a distant dream. Suddenly, Lombard pointed at the water.

"What's that?" he said. "See there? By that big rock? Near the beach. Is it someone swimming?"

"Let's go look!" cried Vera.

When they got to the shore, they found that it was a person. But it wasn't anybody swimming. As they bent down to look, they saw a purple face.

Lombard cried out.

"It's *Armstrong!*"

Slowly, Lombard and Vera turned and looked into each other's eyes.

■the very peak 頂点、頂上　■so far away 遠く離れて　■bend down to look かがんでのぞき込む　■look into each other's eyes お互いの目を見つめ合う

ふたりは頂上まで歩いていくと、そこに立って無言のまま周囲を見まわ
した。ふだんの暮らしが遠くに、まるではるかな夢のように感じられる。す
ると、ロンバードが海のほうを指さした。
　「あれはなんだろう？」と言う。「見えるかい？　あの大きな岩のそばだ
よ。浜辺の近くだ。誰かが泳いでいるのかな？」
　「見にいきましょう！」ヴェラは叫んだ。
　ふたりが海岸に着くと、それは人だとわかった。だが、泳いでいるので
はなかった。かがんでよく見ると、紫色に変色した顔が見えた。

　ロンバードが大声で叫んだ。
　「アームストロングだ！」
　ゆっくりと、ロンバードとヴェラは顔を向けあい、たがいの目をのぞき
こんだ。

Chapter Fourteen

"I see," said Lombard.

Vera said nothing.

"This is the end, Vera."

Vera only looked at the body floating in the water.

"Poor Dr. Armstrong…" she said.

"Oh, now you feel sorry for him, do you?" Lombard said with a cruel laugh.

"Why not?" Vera snapped back. "We ought to bring him back to the house."

"He can stay where he is," said Lombard.

"We should at least move him out of the water so the waves can't take him back out to sea," she said, strangely calm. "Help me."

■feel sorry for ～をかわいそうに思う ■cruel 形 冷酷な、残酷な ■snap back 言い返す ■ought to ～すべきである

第14章

「なるほど、そういうことか」ロンバードが言った。

ヴェラは何も答えない。

「これで終わりだ、ヴェラ」

ヴェラはただ、海に浮かぶ遺体を見つめている。

「かわいそうなアームストロング先生……」彼女は言った。

「へえ、いまになって、かわいそうだと思うのかい？」ロンバードは冷酷な笑みを浮かべた。

「だって、そうでしょ？」ヴェラは言い返した。「家まで運んであげなきゃ」

「そのままにしとけばいいさ」とロンバード。

「せめて水から出して、波にさらわれないようにしてあげるべきよ」ヴェラは奇妙なほど落ち着いている。「手伝ってちょうだい」

"If you like," Lombard said with a cruel smile. He bent over and pulled at the body. Vera leaned against him, helping him. After a while, they got the body out of the water and up onto the sand.

"Satisfied?" asked Lombard, straightening up.

"Quite." Something about Vera's voice warned him. He spun around. His hand went to his pocket for his gun, but it was empty.

Vera pointed the gun at him.

"That's why you wanted to pull the body out of the water! To steal my gun!"

Vera nodded.

Lombard's head raced. He must do something! He wasn't beat yet!

"Look here, dear girl," he said calmly. "Give that gun to me." Suddenly, he jumped at her. Vera pulled the trigger. Lombard crashed onto the beach, dead.

■bend over 前かがみになる ■lean against 〜に寄りかかる ■straighten up 体を起こす、立ち上がる ■Quite.〔相づち・賛成の返事として〕まったくそうだ。そのとおり。 ■spin around 回転する、振り返る ■crash onto 〜に転がる、打ちつける

「まあ、そうしたいんならね」ロンバードは冷ややかに笑いながらそう言うと、かがんで遺体を引きずりはじめた。ヴェラも彼に寄りかかるようにして手伝った。ようやく、ふたりは遺体を水中から砂浜の上まで引きあげた。

　「これで満足かい？」ロンバードが体を起こしながら訊いた。

　「ええ、すっかりね」ヴェラの声の何かに、ロンバードは危険を感じた。あわてて振りかえる。ピストルを取ろうとポケットに手をのばしたが、からっぽだった。

　ヴェラはピストルを彼に向けていた。

　「だから遺体を水から引きあげようなんて言ったのか！　おれからピストルを盗むためだったんだな！」

　ヴェラはうなずいた。

　ロンバードはすばやく考えを巡らせた。なんとかしなくては！　まだ負けたわけじゃないぞ！

　「ねえ、お嬢さん」と穏やかな声を出す。「そのピストルを返してくれよ」そして、いきなりヴェラに飛びかかった。ヴェラがとっさに引き金を引く。ロンバードは砂浜の上にドサリと倒れ、その場で息絶えた。

Vera stood there, not moving. She was shocked at what she had done, yes, but she was so happy! She had done it! She had survived. She was alone on the island... There was no more fear...

*　*　*

The sun was setting when Vera moved at last. She realized she was hungry and sleepy. Tomorrow, perhaps, someone would come from the village and find her. But tonight, she could finally sleep safely.

She walked back to the house. She stopped by the dining room and looked at the table. There were three little soldier boys.

"You're behind the times, my dear!" she said, laughing. She took two soldiers and threw them out the window. Picking up the last one, she said, "You can come with me. We've won!"

She walked slowly up the stairs. Her legs felt heavy, and she was so very tired. She didn't even notice when the gun slipped from her hand.

■at last〔長時間かかって〕やっと、ようやく　■stop by 途中で立ち寄る　■behind the times 時代[時勢]に遅れて　■not even notice 全く気づかない、気にも留めない

ヴェラはそこに立ったまま、身じろぎもしなかった。自分がしたことに
ショックを受けていた。そう、ショックだわ、だけど、なんて幸せなの！
とうとうやったわ！　わたしは生きのびたのよ。島でひとりきり……。もう
何も怖がらなくていい……。

＊　＊　＊

　日が沈みかけた頃、ヴェラはやっと動きだした。お腹がすいたし、とて
も眠い。明日になれば、たぶん村から誰かが来て、自分を見つけてくれる
だろう。でも今夜は、ようやく安心して眠れるのだ。

　ヴェラは家へ戻っていった。ダイニングルームに立ちよって、テーブル
を見る。小さな兵隊の人形が3つあった。

「あなたたち、遅れてるわよ！」彼女は笑った。ふたつの兵隊をつかんで、
窓の外へ投げ捨てる。最後のひとつを取りあげると、「あなたはいっしょに
いらっしゃい。わたしたちは勝ったのよ！」と言った。
　彼女はゆっくりと階段を上がっていった。足が重いし、とてつもなく疲
れていた。手からピストルがすべり落ちたことさえ、気づかなかった。

"What was the last line?" she thought. *"One little soldier boy left all alone…"*

Vera continued to climb the stairs slowly. She thought she felt the presence of someone else in the house.

"Hugo," she thought, "Hugo, is that you?"

Now she was at her door. She went into her room. Her sleepy eyes opened wide at what she saw.

A rope made into a noose hung from the hook in the ceiling. Under it was a chair to stand upon.

"This is what Hugo wanted…" she thought. "The last line… *He went and hanged himself and then there were None.*"

Slowly, like a robot, Vera went to the chair. She stepped onto it. The soldier figure dropped from her hand. She put the noose around her neck. She kicked the chair away.

■feel the presence of ～の存在を感じる　■noose 図 輪なわ、ヌース　■step onto ～に上がる、乗り込む

「詩の最後の行は、どんなだったかしら？」彼女は考えた。「『1人の小さ
な兵隊さんがひとりぼっちになったよ』……」

　ヴェラはのろのろと階段をのぼりつづけた。なんとなく、家の中に誰か
がいるような気がする。

　「ヒューゴー」ふと、そう思う。「ヒューゴー、あなたなの？」

　ようやく自分の部屋だ。彼女は中に入り、そこにあるものを見て、眠い
目を大きく見開いた。

　輪になったロープが、天井のフックからぶらさがっているのだ。その下
には、踏み台にする椅子まで置かれている。

　「これが、ヒューゴーの望みなのね……」と思う。「最後の行はたしか…
…『自分で首をくくって、そして誰もいなくなった』」

　ヴェラはゆっくりと、まるでロボットのように椅子に近づいて、その上
にのぼった。兵隊の人形が手からすべり落ちる。ヴェラは輪を自分の首に
かけた。そして、椅子をけった。

A Document Found by the Captain of the *Emma Jane* Fishing Boat

From the time I was very young, I knew that I was strange. I was born with both an active imagination and a strong desire to hurt and kill things. However, alongside this desire was a strong sense of justice. I hated to harm innocent people or things. This is perhaps why I entered law.

As a judge, I loved to see criminals suffer in court. However, later in my life, I began to want more. Judging wasn't enough—I wanted to *act* upon my desires. I wanted to commit a murder myself. And it must not be an ordinary murder; it must be fantastic, incredible! I wanted to let my imagination run wild.

■desire 图 願望、欲望　■alongside 副 ～と同時に、並行に[して]　■criminal 图 犯罪者　■suffer 動〔肉体的・精神的に〕苦しむ　■act upon ～に従って[基づいて]行動する　■commit a murder 殺人を犯す、人殺しをする　■let one's imagination run wild 想像力に身を委ねる

漁船〈エマ・ジェイン号〉の
船長が発見した文書

　わたしは幼少の頃から、自分がふつうではないことに気づいていた。生まれつき豊かな想像力と、生きものを傷つけたり殺したりしたいという強い欲望があった。しかし、この欲望とともに、強い正義感も持っていた。無実の人間や生きものに危害を加えることには嫌悪を覚えた。おそらくそれが、法律の世界に入った理由だろう。

　判事として、犯罪者が法廷で苦しむのを見るのが好きだった。だが後年になると、さらに欲が強くなってきた。判決を下すだけでは物足りない——欲望に従って行動したい。自分で殺人を犯してみたい。それも、ふつうの殺人ではだめだ。奇想天外で、すばらしいものでなければ！　わたしは自分の想像力を解き放ちたかったのだ。

But how? The idea came to me through a normal conversation. I was speaking with a doctor friend of mine when he mentioned how many murders must happen that the law cannot touch. His example was the death of one elderly woman, whom he suspected was killed by two servants—Rogers and Mrs. Rogers—by not giving her the medicine she needed. With her death, the couple came into a lot of money. That kind of thing was impossible to prove, said my friend, but he was sure it happened all the time.

That was how the whole thing began. I suddenly saw who my victims would be: those guilty of crimes that couldn't be touched by the law. A childish poem came to my head—the one about the ten soldier boys disappearing one by one. I began, secretly, to collect my victims.

■servant 图〔家事を行う〕召使い、使用人　■come into 〔財産などを〕相続する、受け継ぐ　■victim 图 被害者、犠牲者、餌食　■one by one 一人ずつ、一つずつ

しかしどうやって？　いい考えが浮かんだのは、ふだんの会話を通して
だった。友人の医師と話していたとき、法律の手の及ばない殺人がたくさ
んあるにちがいないと、彼が言ったのだ。例として、ひとりの老婦人の死
について話してくれた。彼女はふたりの使用人——ロジャーズ夫妻——に、
必要な薬を与えられずに殺されたのではないかと彼は疑っていた。老婦人
の死によって、夫妻は多額の遺産を手に入れた。このようなことは証明の
しようがないが、しょっちゅうあるにちがいないと友人は語った。

　こうして、すべてが始まった。一瞬にして、わたしの獲物になるべき者
がわかったのだ。それは、法律の手の及ばない犯罪者たちだ。そしてある
童謡が頭の中に浮かんできた——10人の小さな兵隊がひとりずつ消えてい
くという、あの童謡。わたしは密かに自分の獲物を探しはじめた。

To do this, I had a line of conversation that I used with nearly everyone I met. The results were surprising. From a nurse who treated me for an illness, I discovered the case of Dr. Armstrong, who had killed a woman by operating on her while he was drunk. A conversation between two military gentlemen at my club gave me the story of General Macarthur. I heard about Philip Lombard from a man who had recently returned from the Amazon. A middle-aged married woman I met somewhere told me about Emily Brent and her servant girl. I chose Anthony Marston from a large group of people who had committed similar crimes. The story of Mr. Blore came to me from friends at work—lawyers talking rather freely about the Landor case.

Finally, there was the case of Vera Claythorne. It came when I was crossing the Atlantic. Late one night, the only people in the ship's smoking room were myself and a young gentleman named Hugo Hamilton.

He was unhappy, and to forget his unhappiness, he had been drinking. I tried my usual line of conversation and to my great surprise, I got an incredible story.

■treat someone for an illness（人）の病気を治療する ■at work 仕事をして、職場で[に] ■freely 副 率直に、遠慮なく ■Atlantic 图《the ～》大西洋 ■to one's great surprise（人）が大変驚いたことに

その探索のため、人に会うたびに、似たような一連の会話で訊きだそう
とした。結果は驚くべきものだった。病気のとき世話になった看護婦から、
アームストロング医師の事件を知った。彼は酒に酔って手術をし、女性を死
なせたのだ。ふたりの軍人とクラブで話したときには、マッカーサー将軍
の話を聞いた。フィリップ・ロンバードのことは、アマゾンから戻ったば
かりの男から聞かされた。また、あるところで出会った中年の既婚女性は、
エミリー・ブレントと小間使いの娘の話をわたしに語った。アンソニー・
マーストンは、同じような罪を犯した大勢の中から選んだ。ブロアについ
ての情報は、仕事上の友人たちからだった――弁護士たちがランドー事件
について思うところを率直に話してくれたのだ。

　最後に、ヴェラ・クレイソーンの件があった。それは大西洋を横断して
いたときのことだ。夜遅くに船の喫煙室で、ヒューゴー・ハミルトンとい
う青年とふたりきりになった。

　彼は不幸せそうで、その不幸を忘れるために酒を飲んでいた。わたしが
いつもの会話を試してみると、驚いたことに、信じられないような話を聞
くことができたのだ。

"You're right," he said. "Murder isn't what most people think. I've actually known a *murderess*. And what's more, I was in love with her! She did it, I believe, for me! Not that I ever dreamed she would ever do such a thing…She took a boy out to sea to drown!"

"Are you sure she did it?" I asked.

"Yes. I knew the moment I looked at her. What she didn't realize was that I loved that boy…"

I found my tenth victim in the form of a Mr. Morris, a bad character indeed. He dealt mainly in drugs. Once, he successfully got a young woman addicted to drugs, and she ended up killing herself.

I am old, and I know I do not have much longer to live, so I put my plan into action. I bought Soldier Island through Morris, who was very good at keeping my identity hidden. I then studied the information I had gathered on my "soldier boys" and created a suitable bait for each. Everybody took the bait. They all arrived on Soldier Island on August 8, myself included.

■murderess 图〈古〉女性の殺人者　■what's more　その上　■deal in〔人・店などが〕～の取引をする　■addicted to〔薬や娯楽の〕中毒になっている、夢中になっている　■put one's plan into action　計画を実行に移す　■identity 图〔人やものの〕正体、身元　■bait 图餌、誘惑する[心を引く]もの

「そのとおりですよ」彼は言った。「殺人は、多くの人が考えてるような
もんじゃない。ぼくは実際、人を殺した女を知っています。それどころか、
その女を愛していたんですよ！　きっと、ぼくのためにやったんだ！　そん
なことをするなんて、夢にも思わなかった……。小さな男の子を海へ連れ
だして、溺れさせるなんて！」

　「たしかにその女がやったのかね？」わたしは尋ねた。

　「そうです。目を合わせた瞬間、わかりました。でも、ぼくがその子を愛
していたことに、彼女は気づかなかったんだ……」

　10人目の獲物として見いだしたのはモリスだった。まぎれもない悪党だ。
おもに麻薬の売人をしていた。以前、ある娘をわざと中毒にしたことがあ
り、その娘はついに自殺してしまった。

　わたしは年老い、もうそれほど長くは生きられないとわかっている。だ
から、計画を実行に移すことにした。まず、モリスを通して兵隊島を買っ
た。わたしの身元を隠すことなど、モリスにとってはわけないことだ。そ
れから、わたしの「小さな兵隊」たちについて集めた情報を調べて、それぞ
れにぴったりの餌をこしらえた。すると誰もがその餌に食いついた。わた
しも含めて、全員が8月8日に兵隊島にやってきたのだ。

I had already taken care of Morris. He suffered from stomach problems, and the night before I left London I gave him a drug that I said did wonders for my own stomach. He took the drug, and he died.

I carefully planned the order of death on the island. The least guilty would die first, so that they would not suffer from the fear and mental stress that the guiltier had to live through. Anthony Marston and Mrs. Rogers died first. Marston was born without any idea of morals, of right or wrong. There was no evil in what he did, it was pure ignorance. Mrs. Rogers, I have no doubt, had been influenced to kill by her husband.

It was easy to put cyanide into Marston's glass. As for Mrs. Rogers, I slipped a deadly amount of sleeping medicine into her brandy when Rogers set her glass down on a table. General Macarthur met his end very quietly. He did not hear me come up behind him. I had to choose my time for leaving the terrace carefully, but everything was successful.

■take care of ～を殺す［始末する］ ■do wonders for ～に驚くべき効果を発揮する ■so that ～できるように ■ignorance 图 無知、知らないこと ■have no doubt ～ ということを確信している［少しも疑わない］ ■meet one's end 最期を遂げる、死ぬ ■come up behind ～の背後から近づいてくる

モリスのほうは、すでに始末しておいた。彼は胃の具合が悪かったので、わたしはロンドンをたつ前夜に、自分の胃には驚くほどよく効いたと言って、薬を与えたのだ。彼はその薬を飲んで息絶えた。

　わたしは島での死の順番を慎重に計画した。もっとも罪の軽い者が、いちばんに死ぬ。より罪深い者が耐えねばならない恐怖や精神的ストレスを受けずにすむようにだ。アンソニー・マーストンと、ミセス・ロジャーズが最初に死んだ。マーストンは生まれながらに、道徳や善悪について考える力が欠けていた。彼のしたことには邪悪さがない。純粋に無知によるものだ。ミセス・ロジャーズは、夫にそそのかされてやったにちがいない。

　マーストンのグラスに青酸カリを入れるのは簡単だった。ミセス・ロジャーズについては、ロジャーズが彼女のブランデーのグラスをテーブルに置いたときに、致死量の睡眠薬をそっと入れたのだ。マッカーサー将軍は、じつに静かに最期を迎えた。わたしが背後から近づくのも聞こえなかっただろう。テラスを離れる時間を慎重に選ばねばならなかったが、すべてはうまくいった。

As I expected, the three deaths caused a search of the island, and we discovered that there was nobody else on the island but ourselves. This created suspicion. I had planned to seek an ally, and I chose Dr. Armstrong, since he already knew me from before. He suspected Lombard and I said I agreed. I told him I had a plan with which we might be able to make the murderer reveal himself.

I killed Rogers on the morning of the 10th. He was cutting sticks and did not notice me behind him. In the confusion that rose after finding Rogers's body, I went into Lombard's room and stole his gun. I knew he would have one, because I had told Morris to make sure Lombard brought one.

At breakfast I slipped my last bit of sleeping medicine into Miss Brent's coffee when I was filling her cup. We left her in the dining room, and I slipped in there a few minutes later. She was so sleepy it was easy to inject her with the rest of the cyanide. Putting the bee in the window was rather childish, but it pleased me to stay as close to the rhyme as possible.

■ally 図 協力者、支持者 ■last bit of わずかに残った〜 ■inject 〜 with 〜に…を注射する ■please 動〔人を〕満足させる

予想どおり、3人の死によって島の捜索が行われ、島にはわれわれ以外誰
もいないことがはっきりした。このことが、おたがいのあいだに疑惑をも
たらした。わたしは協力者を求める計画だったので、アームストロング医
師を選んだ。以前からわたしのことを知っていたからだ。彼はロンバード
を疑っていたので、わたしも賛成だと言った。そして作戦があるともちか
け、これで犯人の正体を暴けるかもしれないと説得した。

　10日の朝に、ロジャーズを殺した。彼は薪を割っていたので、背後にい
るわたしに気づかなかった。ロジャーズの遺体を発見したあとの混乱の中
で、ロンバードの部屋へ忍びこんでピストルを盗みだした。彼がピストル
を持っていることはわかっていた。ロンバードにピストルを持ってこさせ
るようにと、わたしがモリスに言ったからだ。
　朝食中、ミス・ブレントのカップにコーヒーをついでいるときに、残って
いた睡眠薬をこっそり入れた。みなで彼女をダイニングルームに残したが、
わたしは数分後に戻っていった。彼女はひどく眠そうだったので、残って
いた青酸カリを注射するのはたやすかった。窓にハチを放したのは子ども
じみた真似だが、できるだけ詩の内容に近づけることができて、わたしは
満足だった。

After this, I suggested that we search the house. I had hidden the gun in a safe place—in a tin of biscuits at the bottom of a pile of canned food in the kitchen. It was then that I told Armstrong we had to carry out my plan. The plan was this: I must appear to be the next victim. Once I was dead, I would be free to move about the house and spy on the unknown murderer.

Armstrong liked the idea. We carried it out that evening, and it worked. Miss Claythorne started screaming when she found the seaweed I had placed in her room. All the men ran upstairs, and I stayed in the drawing room to put on my judge's costume and a little red mud on my forehead. The doctor acted out his part, and they carried me into my room, believing I was dead. Nobody worried about me after that. They were all too afraid of each other.

I had arranged to meet Armstrong outside the house that night at a quarter to two. I took him up by the edge of the cliff, saying that we could watch the house from up there. He never suspected me.

■tin 图〈英〉〔缶詰の〕缶 ■pile of 《a ~》〈話〉山のような、山積みの ■appear to be ~であるように見える[思われる] ■spy on ~を探る、偵察する ■mud 图泥、ぬかるみ ■act out 〔劇の場面・役を〕演じる ■at a quarter to ~時15分前に

このあと、わたしは家を捜索するよう提案した。ピストルは安全な場所
に隠してあった——台所に山積みされた缶詰の下にあるビスケットの缶の
中だ。そのときアームストロングに、作戦を実行しようと言ったのだ。そ
の作戦とは、以下のようなものだ。まず、わたしを次の犠牲者のように見
せかける。わたしが死んだことにすれば、自由に家を動きまわって、アン
ノウンという謎の殺人者を探しだすことができるだろう。

　アームストロングはこの思いつきが気に入ったようだ。さっそくその夜
に実行し、じつにうまくいった。ミス・クレイソーンは、わたしが彼女の
部屋にぶらさげた海草を見るなり、悲鳴をあげはじめた。男たちがみな階
段を駆けあがると、わたしは客間に残って判事の格好をし、額に赤い泥を
少し塗りつけた。医師が自分の役をうまく演じたので、みなはわたしが死
んだと信じこんで、わたしを部屋に運んだ。これで、もう誰もわたしのこ
とは気にかけなくなった。みな、おたがいをひどく恐れていたからだ。

　アームストロングとは、その夜の2時15分前に、外で会う手はずになっ
ていた。わたしは彼を崖のふちへ連れていった。そこからなら家を見張れ
るからと言ったのだ。彼はわたしのことを少しも疑わなかった。

Then I looked over the cliff and cried out, "Is that a cave? Look, there!" Armstrong leaned over and I pushed him over the edge into the sea. He ought to have known better—the next line of the rhyme is "*A red herring swallowed one...*" He certainly took the red herring.

I returned to the house. It must have been my steps that Blore heard. After a few minutes, I stepped out again, making enough noise to make sure someone *would* hear me and follow. I went around the house and climbed back in through the dining room window, which I had left open. I went back to my room and assumed my pose on my bed as a dead man. As I expected, they searched the house again.

The next day was the day that excited me the most. Three people were so afraid of each other that anything might happen, *and one of them had a gun!* I watched them from the windows of the house. When Blore came up alone, I had the big bear ready. I dropped it on him, and that was the end of Blore.

■know better もっと分別がある ■left open 〔ドア・窓などが〕開いたままになっている ■dead man 图《a ～》死者、死人

それから、わたしは崖をのぞきこんで、こう叫んだ。「あれは洞窟かな？ほら、あそこだよ！」アームストロングが身を乗りだしたので、わたしは彼を崖のふちから海へ突きとばした。彼はもっと分別を持つべきだった——童謡の次の行は「燻製のニシンにのまれて……」だったではないか。燻製のニシンにだまされる猟犬のように、まさに彼もだまされたのだ。

　わたしは家に戻った。ブロアが耳にしたのは、その足音だったにちがいない。数分後、わたしはふたたび部屋を出て、誰かが聞きつけて後を追うように、わざと音をたてて歩いた。家に沿って歩くと、先にあけておいたダイニングルームの窓によじのぼり、また中へ入った。すぐに自分の部屋へ戻り、ベッドの中で死人のふりをした。予想どおり、彼らはふたたび家の中を捜索しだした。

　翌日は、もっとも興奮を感じる一日だった。3人はおたがいを非常に恐れているので、何が起きてもおかしくない。しかも、ひとりはピストルを持っているのだ！　わたしは家の窓から彼らを見張っていた。ブロアがひとりでこちらへやってきたので、大きなクマを用意した。クマをブロアの上に落とすと、それが彼の最期になった。

From my window I saw Vera Claythorne shoot Lombard. As soon as she did that, I set up her room with the noose. What followed was an interesting psychological experiment. Would a week spent in constant fear, combined with the guilt of shooting a man, combined with the guilt of killing Cyril push her over the edge and cause her to kill herself? I thought it would, and I was right. Vera Claythorne hanged herself as I watched, hidden in the shadows of her closet.

And now? I will finish writing this, and I will put this letter in a bottle and throw it in the sea. Why? Because I want someone to know that I did all this. I have that very human desire for people to know just how clever I was.

After I throw this bottle into the sea, I will get the gun, which Vera dropped on the stairs on the way to her room. I will loosely tie the black, elastic string that hangs from my glasses to the gun. I will loop this string around the door handle, then I will lie on top of my glasses. Holding the gun with a cloth so as to keep only Vera's fingerprints on the gun, I will shoot myself in the head. When this happens, my hand will fall away and let go of the gun. The elastic string will pull back, pulling the gun too. The gun will hit the door and drop. It will lie there, as if someone else had shot me.

■set up　〜を配置する、準備する　■constant　形 絶えず続く、くり返される
■combined with　〜と組み合わさって、〜と相まって　■elastic string　ゴムひも
■loop　動 〜を輪（状）にする、結ぶ　■fingerprint　名 指紋　■fall away 〔物が〕ずり落ちる

　A Document Found by the Captain of the Emma Jane Fishing Boat

部屋の窓から、ヴェラ・クレイソーンがロンバードを撃つのが見えた。ヴェラが撃ってすぐに、わたしは彼女の部屋に首つり用の輪をぶらさげた。そのあとは、興味深い心理学の実験だった。1週間の絶え間ない恐怖と、男を撃ち殺した罪の意識、そしてシリルを殺した罪悪感が合わされば、彼女は正気を失って自殺するだろうか？　するだろうと、わたしは思った。そして、そのとおりになった。ヴェラ・クレイソーンは、クローゼットの陰に隠れるわたしの目の前で首をつったのだ。

　では、これからどうするのか？　この手紙を書きおえたら、瓶に入れて海へ投げこむつもりだ。なぜか？　わたしがこのすべてを成し遂げたということを、誰かに知ってもらいたいからだ。自分の頭のよさを人々に認めてもらいたいという、なんとも人間らしい願望が、わたしにもあるのだろう。

　瓶を海に投げいれたら、ピストルを手にとる。ヴェラが部屋へ行くときに階段で落としたものだ。眼鏡に取りつけた黒いゴムひもを、ピストルにゆるく結びつける。このひもをドアノブに巻きつけておき、ベッドで眼鏡の上に横になる。ピストルについたヴェラの指紋が消えないように、布で覆ってピストルを持ち、自分の頭を撃ちぬく。そうすると手がずり落ちて、ピストルを放す。そこでゴムひもが縮んでピストルを引っぱり、ピストルはドアにぶつかって床に落ちる。他の誰かがわたしを撃ったかのように、ピストルはそこに残りつづける。

When the sea goes down, the boats will come, and our deaths will be discovered. My Soldier Island mystery will be complete.

Signed:

Lawrence Wargrave

■go down 〔風などが〕収まる　■complete 動~を完成する、仕上げる

海の波が静まれば、ボートがやってきて、われわれの遺体を発見するだろう。こうして、わたしの兵隊島の謎が完成するのだ。

　　　署名
　　　　ロレンス・ウォーグレイヴ

English **C**onversational **A**bility **T**est
国際英語会話能力検定

● E-CATとは…

英語が話せるようになるための
テストです。インターネット
ベースで、30分であなたの発
話力をチェックします。

www.ecatexam.com

● iTEP®とは…

世界各国の企業、政府機関、アメリカの大学
300校以上が、英語能力判定テストとして採用。
オンラインによる90分のテストで文法、リー
ディング、リスニング、ライティング、スピー
キングの5技能をスコア化。iTEP®は、留学、就
職、海外赴任などに必要な、世界に通用する英
語力を総合的に評価する画期的なテストです。

www.itepexamjapan.com

[IBC対訳ライブラリー]
英語で読むそして誰もいなくなった

2020年3月4日　第1刷発行

原著者　　アガサ・クリスティー

発行者　　浦　　晋亮

発行所　　IBCパブリッシング株式会社
　　　　　〒162-0804 東京都新宿区中里町29番3号 菱秀神楽坂ビル9F
　　　　　Tel. 03-3513-4511　Fax. 03-3513-4512
　　　　　www.ibcpub.co.jp

印刷所　　株式会社シナノパブリッシングプレス
CDプレス　株式会社ケーエヌコーポレーションジャパン

© IBC Publishing, Inc. 2020

Printed in Japan

ISBN978-4-7946-0619-8